Baptism in the Spirit

Baptism in the Spirit

Luke-Acts and the Dunn Debate

WILLIAM P. ATKINSON

PICKWICK *Publications* · Eugene, Oregon

BAPTISM IN THE SPIRIT
Luke-Acts and the Dunn Debate

A proportion of the material in this book has previously been published in the following articles, and is reproduced here with the permission of the publishers: "Pentecostal Responses to Dunn's Baptism in the Holy Spirit: Luke-Acts." *JPT* 6 (1995) 87–131. © Sheffield Academic Press Limited, 1995.

"Pentecostal Responses to Dunn's Baptism in the Holy Spirit: Pauline Literature." *JPT* 7 (1995) 49–72. © Sheffield Academic Press Limited, 1995.

"The Prior Work of the Spirit in Luke's Portrayal." Australasian Pentecostal Studies 5-6 (2002) 107–14. Online: http://webjournals.alphacrucis.edu.au/. © 2010 APS.

Pickwick Publications
An Imprint of Wipf and Stock Publishers
199 W. 8th Ave., Suite 3
Eugene, OR 97401

www.wipfandstock.com

ISBN 13: 978-1-60899-971-2

Cataloguing-in-Publication data:

Atkinson, William P., 1961—.

Baptism in the Spirit : Luke-Acts and the Dunn debate / William P. Atkinson.

x + 154 pp. ; 23 cm. Includes bibliographical references and indexes.

ISBN 13: 978-1-60899-971-2

1. Baptism in the Holy Spirit—Biblical teaching. 2. Dunn, James D. G., 1939–. 3. Pentecostalism. I. Title.

BS680.H56 A84 2011

Manufactured in the U.S.A.

Contents

Foreword

IN 1970, James D. G. Dunn's University of Cambridge PhD dissertation was published as *Baptism in the Holy Spirit*, beginning the debate that is the subject of this book. For over a decade, it lay neglected by Pentecostals as they were nonresponsive to Dunn's thesis that the baptism in the Holy Spirit occurred at and, in fact, effected conversion in the believer. That changed in 1984 with the emergence of the next generation of Pentecostal scholars and, particularly, with the publication of Roger Stronstad's *The Charismatic Theology of St. Luke*. The strong works of Robert P. Menzies and James B. Shelton would shortly follow. Also in 1984, Howard M. Ervin weighed in again with a *seriatim* response to Dunn's work.[1] On the other side of the Atlantic, David Petts and the early Max Turner would make important contributions to the debate with Dunn. These scholars, and more, you are about to be introduced to through this excellent work by the Rev. Dr. William P. Atkinson, Associate Research Fellow at the London School of Theology and Associate Minister of Braintree Elim Pentecostal Church (United Kingdom).

It gives me great pleasure to introduce to North American biblical scholarship the author of the award-winning book, *The "Spiritual-Death" of Jesus: A Pentecostal Investigation* (Leiden: Brill, 2009). With equally thorough research, careful analysis, and nuanced commentary, Dr. Atkinson has now turned his pen to this debate with Dunn, which is still lively after forty years.

I am especially impressed by his balanced approach to Dunn's critics. While siding with them when they are correct, he does not hesitate to label their arguments *weak*, *misguided*, or *ill-founded* when deserving.

---

1. Ervin, a neo-Pentecostal, had published *These Are Not Drunken, As Ye Suppose* in 1968 (revised as *Spirit-Baptism: A Biblical Investigation* in 1987). At the time Dunn wrote, Ervin's book was the best exegetical defense of the Pentecostal position. But although it was more than adequate against Unger, Hoekema, Gromacki and the like, Dunn's work ramped the debate to another level.

Foreword

And he sides with Dunn—when he believes he is correct. These disarming features, combined with the irenic spirit that pervades the work, will no doubt win over many readers, although Atkinson confesses that he writes for the edification of the Pentecostal and not to persuade non-Pentecostals.

As you may have guessed, by culling and amassing the strongest arguments of Dunn's critics, little by little Atkinson effectively erodes Dunn's thesis. Well, not quite. The Pauline corpus—with its silence on what Luke stresses—still presents a problem to the Pentecostal thesis, but Atkinson's novel handling of this provides a resolution. By carefully considering the contributions of the three major New Testament writers—Luke, Paul, and John—he successfully synthesizes a theology while respecting the individual voices of each writer—something that Dunn has been unwilling to do. It is not so much that Atkinson rebuts Dunn; rather, he provides a superior perspective of the biblical writers.

Although Dr. Atkinson writes with the acumen of a scholar, he also writes with the heart of a pastor. With fellow pastors in mind, as well as interested laypersons, he crafts the book to make it accessible to them: heavy technical jargon is avoided; Greek words are both transliterated and translated into English; helpful summaries occur at the end of sections and chapters; and principal arguments of the debaters are clearly restated.

Through this work, Atkinson demonstrates that Luke taught that new believers should expect and receive the baptism in the Holy Spirit, which provides power to witness and serve, and they should receive urgent attention if it is not forthcoming. With this new contribution to Pentecostal literature, I see no reason why any Christian leader would oppose such an experience. The baptism in the Holy Spirit is biblical, reasonable, and responsible. This may not have been clear in 1970; it most certainly is now.

Robert W. Graves
President, The Foundation for Pentecostal Scholarship
September 2010

Acknowledgments

I OWE A HUGE debt of gratitude to Max Turner. It was he who more than anyone else taught me how to think critically about theology. He supervised the MA dissertation, at London Bible College in 1992, that is the kernel within this book; and it was he who first arranged for that dissertation to be published in *JPT* once I had submitted it. Anybody reading this book will discover that I do not agree with Turner entirely concerning Luke-Acts but I acknowledge, without hesitation, that his contribution to our knowledge of Lukan pneumatology is immense. His contribution to my personal acquaintance with Lukan pneumatology is immeasurable.

The other person whose help I wish to acknowledge with immense gratitude is Robert Graves. I greatly appreciate his originally suggesting that I now update and expand this material so that it might be publishable in book form. He has given me unstinting personal encouragement and practical help, and has put certain resources of the Foundation for Pentecostal Scholarship at my disposal. Robert, I am most grateful.

I am grateful to the editors of *JPT* and *Australasian Pentecostal Studies* for their permission to reprint in this book content from articles published previously in their journals.

Finally, I wish to place on record my gratitude to Robin Parry, my editor, and all involved staff at Wipf and Stock for their help in bringing this work to publication.

Abbreviations

1 En.	*1 Enoch*
JEPTA	*Journal of the European Pentecostal Theological Association*
JPT	*Journal of Pentecostal Theology*
JPTSup	Journal of Pentecostal Theology Supplement Series
JSNTSup	Journal for the Study of the New Testament Supplement Series
Jub.	*Jubilees*
LXX	Septuagint
NICNT	New International Commentary on the New Testament
Num. Rab.	*Numbers Rabbah*
Pss. Sol.	*Psalms of Solomon*
Q	*Quelle* (postulated non-Markan source behind Matt and Luke)
1QS	A scroll from Cave 1 at Qumran: *The Community Rule*
T. Jud.	*Testament of Judah*
T. Levi	*Testament of Levi*

1

The Dunn Debate and Its Inception

INTRODUCTION

THIS BOOK IS WRITTEN primarily for my fellow Pentecostals.[1] It is about that central, treasured doctrine of ours: baptism in the Holy Spirit. My aim is to offer an explanation and defense of the doctrine, before also offering some brief practical applications of it for church life today. My defense of the doctrine, unsurprisingly, will focus on the scriptural foundation on which it has been built. As the subtitle of this book indicates, I will be focusing, as so many Pentecostals have before me, on Luke's Gospel and his other work, the Acts of the Apostles. However, chapter 4 will bring Luke's voice alongside those of other key New Testament authors on the subject. My subtitle also mentions the *Dunn Debate*. While Pentecostals and non-Pentecostals have, generally, disagreed over the meaning of the phrase *baptized in the Holy Spirit* throughout Pentecostalism's history, those familiar with academic writing on this subject will know that the modern phase of the debate dates back to the publication in 1970 of a book by James Dunn titled *Baptism in the Holy Spirit*.[2] This book vigorously challenged the Pentecostal understanding of the New Testament on this subject. Several Pentecostals in the academic world have responded to Dunn's thesis in writing. A study of their debate with Dunn provides an excellent way of consider-

1. It is an updating, expansion, and significant development of my earlier articles: "Pentecostal Responses to Dunn's *Baptism in the Holy Spirit*: Luke-Acts" and "Pentecostal responses to Dunn's *Baptism in the Holy Spirit*: Pauline Literature," both published in *JPT*, and "The Prior Work of the Spirit in Luke's Portrayal," published in *Australasian Pentecostal Studies*.

2. Originally a doctoral dissertation; published in 1970 in London by SCM; subsequently reprinted in 1977 as a Westminster Press "Classic." For a brief survey of the debate, see Mittelstadt, *Reading Luke-Acts*, ch. 2: "The Dunn Factor."

ing the best of current thought from Pentecostals about baptism in the Spirit. As I consider the Pentecostal contributions to the debate, I will weigh the strengths and weaknesses of each contribution. Taking the strongest features of each argument, and adding certain observations of my own, enables a robust defense—and explanation—of Spirit baptism as it is understood by the keenest Pentecostal minds today.

In writing this book, however, I do not primarily seek to persuade non-Pentecostals or ex-Pentecostals to change their views. If the likes of Stronstad and Menzies have not convinced people like Dunn, it is not very likely that my own contribution will achieve this! My aims are somewhat more modest. I hope to show my fellow Pentecostals that there are good reasons, in the face of strong arguments against our views, for continuing to hold them. I aim to indicate that the Pentecostal position is cogent and attractive.

I also have a more general aim. I trust that this book will help to bridge the divide that exists between academic theological study and current Pentecostal church practice and mission. In my own context, this divide is still wide and deep: it needs all the long, strong bridges that can be mustered! I hope to show that academic theological study does have its uses, and that those uses are relevant to Pentecostals who, for whatever reason do not intend to or do not have the opportunity to en-gage in such study themselves. With this in mind, I try to write in a way that is reasonably accessible for people who may not be used to scholarly language. I keep technical terminology to a minimum, transliterate and translate all the Greek I use, and confine all quotations of non-biblical ancient sources to footnotes.

Pentecostalism and Spirit Baptism

If humanity's history on this earth continues long enough, then per-haps it will look back at the twentieth century and judge that church history's greatest single phenomenon was the extraordinary appearance, rise, growth, and spread of world Pentecostalism. With this growth and spread of Pentecostalism, of course, has come an increase in the extent to which it is known by those outside its ranks. We Pentecostals are known for our worship: its vibrancy, informality, and even excitability. We are known for our eschatological expectancy and for our expectancy in the here and now of miraculous interventions from on high, including those mediated through gifted individuals. We are known for our evangelistic fervor (though many of us know in ourselves that we are not as fervent as we ought to be). But among these distinctives and characteristics one feature stands out above all others: our belief in and valuing of "the baptism in the Holy Spirit." Such is our commitment to this doctrine and practice that Frank Macchia can write: "I do not think it is an exaggeration to say that this understanding of Spirit baptism has imprinted itself on the Pentecostal psyche as the crown jewel of Pentecostal distinctives."[3] For many of us, this "crown jewel" is the *sine qua non* of Pentecostalism.[4]

Spirit baptism is not perceived uniformly across the whole of Pentecostalism. Nevertheless, Macchia's brief characterization of Spirit baptism as "an empowerment for ministry distinct from regeneration or initiation into Christ" is sufficiently central to Pentecostal self-understanding for him to write, "enough have understood Spirit baptism as a postconversion charismatic experience to make this view of the doctrine distinctly Pentecostal."[5] Macchia writes here of baptism in the Spirit as "distinct from regeneration" and as "postconversion." J. Rodman Williams' analysis combines these thoughts: "Pentecostals often speak of baptism in the Spirit as being distinct from and subsequent to salvation," but takes care immediately to point out that "this does not necessarily mean a chronologically separate experience." Rather, "the important point for the Pentecostal is not chronological but logical subsequence."[6] This is the definition of baptism in the Holy Spirit that I shall apply throughout this book (while obviously at times referring to other people's definitions): it is a charismatic empowering for Christian service distinct from and thus, potentially, chronologically subsequent to initial regenerating faith in Christ. I will also call this the Pentecostal doctrine of *subsequence*.

---

3. Macchia, *Baptized in the Spirit*, 20. Nevertheless, Vinson Synan is right to observe, "the baptism in the Holy Spirit—with its accompanying gifts and graces—doesn't belong only to the Pentecostals. It belongs to the whole Body of Christ" (Synan, *An Eyewitness Remembers*, 29).

4. Baptism in the Spirit stands as one of the features in the typical Pentecostal "foursquare gospel" of Jesus as "Savior, Healer, Baptizer in the Holy Spirit, and Soon-Coming King," from which central set of doctrines flow Pentecostals' enthusiasm for evangelism, miracles, Spirit baptism, and preaching on the second coming of Christ. Dayton opines of Pentecostalism that, "these four themes are well-nigh universal within the movement" (Dayton, *Theological Roots*, 23). In some traditions, the full gospel is fivefold, with Sanctification added.

5. Macchia, *Baptized in the Spirit*, 20.

6. Williams, "Baptism in the Holy Spirit," 43.

This doctrine has not only proved to be characteristic of typical Pentecostalism and one of Pentecostalism's main distinctives; it has also proved to be highly debatable. This book considers the subject by studying a certain aspect of that debate. The aspect in question is the one that comes into focus when baptism in the Spirit is considered through two "lenses." The first of these lenses is the writing on the subject known in scholarly circles as Luke-Acts, and the second lens is the writing on the subject by James Dunn. I will turn to Professor Dunn shortly, but first a word about Luke-Acts.

Spirit Baptism and Luke-Acts

It is perhaps an unfortunate though understandable feature of the standard canonical order of the Gospels and Acts in our New Testaments that Luke and Acts are separated by John. This feature means that some readers of the New Testament may fail to observe that Luke and Acts are two companion volumes by the same author.[7] However, once this feature is acknowledged, many areas of common ground between the two volumes come to light. One of these is Luke's[8] particular interest in the Holy Spirit. Another is his interest, evidenced especially but not exclusively in Acts, in the growing mission of the church that spread Jesus' message internationally. These twin interests combine. Luke related the work of the Holy Spirit to the evangelistic mission of Christ's followers, and he did this in a more sustained and focused way than any other New Testament author.[9]

---

7. This conclusion is almost universally acknowledged by scholars. Ben Witherington III writes of "the considerable linguistic, grammatical, thematic, and theological evidence that these volumes both come from the same hand" (Witherington, *Acts*, 5).

8. The traditional view of the authorship of Luke-Acts is, of course, that it is by Doctor Luke, the sometime travelling companion of the apostle Paul (Col 4:14; Phlm 24). I have no reason to doubt this view, though it does raise some difficult questions that I will address in chapter 4. From the internal evidence of Luke-Acts, Witherington draws the conclusion that its author is a second generation Christian whose mother tongue is Greek and who has received a good Greco-Roman education. While he does not seem to know Aramaic or Hebrew, and is therefore almost certainly not from Israel, he does display a strong familiarity with the Greek Old Testament translation (the Septuagint [LXX]) and so has perhaps been a God-fearer attached to Jewish synagogues for some time before his conversion to Christ. Witherington indulges in the speculation that Luke may have been a convert of Paul, perhaps in Troas or Philippi (Witherington, *Acts*, 52–54, and 53 n. 193).

9. Note the title of Penney's work on the subject: *The Missionary Emphasis of Lukan Pneumatology*.

As part of his interest in the Holy Spirit, Luke described several occasions when, as he put it, people "received" the Holy Spirit. He used several terms for Spirit reception,[10] one of which, that he repeated, was "being baptized with the Holy Spirit." Outside Luke-Acts, the phrase only appears in verses parallel and roughly parallel to Luke 3:16 (Matt 3:11; Mark 1:8; John 1:33) and in 1 Corinthians 12:13, the translation of which is disputed, especially by Pentecostals (see chapter 4). Given Luke's twin interests in the Holy Spirit and in evangelistic witness and his repeated use of the phrase "baptized with the Holy Spirit," it is hardly surprising that we Pentecostals have turned repeatedly to Luke-Acts for primary biblical data concerning our distinctive doctrine of Spirit baptism.[11] This interest in Luke's works has been so consistent and extensive that Luke-Acts has often been called a "canon-within-the-canon" for Pentecostalism. Such is the volume of Pentecostal writing on Luke-Acts that Mittelstadt's excellent bibliography of Pentecostal writing on Luke-Acts, published in 2010, extends to 35 pages.[12]

Part of this interest in and reliance on Luke-Acts comes to light when the debate with James Dunn concerning baptism in the Spirit is studied. Dunn himself wrote his famous book *Baptism in the Holy Spirit* as a study of the whole New Testament on the subject. However, when Pentecostals came to respond to his thesis, most of them confined their responses to the study of Luke-Acts. This is not true of them all. Howard Ervin and David Petts, in particular, engage with Dunn's reading of Paul, and I will refer to their findings briefly in chapter 4. Ervin, in fact, tackles Dunn's exegesis of the whole New Testament.[13] However, the bulk of Pentecostal debate with Dunn has been "fought on the battle-ground" of Luke-Acts. With this in mind, I am going to restrict most of this book to Lukan issues. I will stray briefly in chapter 4 to studies of 1 Corinthians

10. Luke used such terms as being "filled with the Spirit," "receiving the Spirit," being "baptized with the Spirit," the Spirit "coming upon," "falling upon," being "poured out" upon, and God "giving" the Spirit. He used these, generally, to refer to the same overall experience and effect in a person's life. See further discussion in chapter 3.

11. It is worth noting that the noun phrases "baptism in (or with) the Holy Spirit" and the shorter, rather unlovely "Spirit baptism" do not appear in Luke-Acts, or anywhere else in the Bible. Only the verb "baptize" is used in this precise context.

12. Mittelstadt, *Reading Luke-Acts*, 170–205.

13. There are brief articles in *JPT* 19 (2010) studying Paul (by Janet Meyer Everts) and John (by John Christopher Thomas). Dunn replies to these in "Baptism Again."

12:13 and John 20:22, for reasons that I hope will make sense by then. Otherwise, Luke's writings will be the main focus of our study.

Spirit Baptism and James Dunn

James ("Jimmie") Dunn, Emeritus Lightfoot Professor of Divinity at the University of Durham, is one of Britain's most prominent and influential New Testament theologians in our generation. It is beyond doubt that, through both the students he has personally taught and those preparing for ministry who have read his many books, he has affected the beliefs and biblical understanding of a good proportion of today's Christians. His publishing list is both prodigious and prestigious, and it covers a wide range of the key issues that the New Testament raises for academicians and church members. Only history or eternity will tell which of his many works has had the most impact, but for us Pentecostals one book stands out in its prominence: Dunn's first monograph—his published doctoral research—studying baptism in the Holy Spirit as understood by Pentecostals on the one hand and the New Testament on the other.

As I wrote in a previous section, the modern phase of the Pentecostal debate surrounding Luke-Acts goes back to this book, which I will simply call *Baptism*. Max Turner, an active participant in the debate, calls Dunn's work "one of the most significant books to be written on New Testament pneumatology this century."[14] In this study, Dunn engages with the Pentecostal doctrine of subsequence.[15] Dunn questions this belief: "Does the NT mean by baptism in the Holy Spirit what the Pentecostal understands the phrase to mean? Is baptism in the Holy Spirit to be separated from conversion-initiation,[16] and is the beginning of Christian life to be thus divided up into distinct stages? Is Spirit-baptism something essentially different from becoming a Christian, so that even a Christian of many years' standing may never have been baptized in the Spirit?"[17] On this issue, Dunn reveals his position at the outset: "I hope to show that

---

14. Turner, *Holy Spirit and Spiritual Gifts*, 19, referring, of course, to the twentieth century.

15. *Baptism in the Holy Spirit* is subtitled *A Re-examination of the New Testament Teaching on the Gift of the Spirit in Relation to Pentecostalism Today.*

16. Dunn uses the composite term *conversion-initiation* consistently for the "total event of becoming a Christian" (Dunn, *Baptism*, 7), including both the inward subjective (conversion) and ritual external (initiation) aspects.

17. Dunn, *Baptism*, 3.

for the writers of the NT the baptism in or gift of the Spirit was part of the event (or process) of becoming a Christian . . . ; that it was the chief element in conversion-initiation so that only those who had received the Spirit could be called Christians."[18] It will be immediately apparent to anyone who is not yet familiar with Dunn's work that he engages in some sharp criticism of this Pentecostal doctrine, though in fact he does so from a position of respect for many aspects of Pentecostalism. It is not surprising, given the sharpness of Dunn's critique, that many Pentecostals of a more academic bent have replied to him in print, thus spurring the debate that is considered in this book.

It is greatly to James Dunn's credit that this doctoral dissertation should still, forty years later, be the subject of international debate: a special session of the Society of Biblical Literature conference in New Orleans in November 2009 was devoted to the work and brought out as a series of articles in *JPT* volume 19 (published in 2010). This debate has not, it must be admitted, "raged" continuously for those forty years. The main focus occurred in the first thirty. Nevertheless, one can guess that the average doctoral student would be thrilled to imagine that his or her dissertation might cause as much long-lasting stir as Dunn's has achieved. Dunn's hope, expressed retrospectively after those forty years, was that his work would inspire discussion among both sacramentalists and Pentecostals. The former hope has remained unfulfilled,[19] but Dunn cannot justifiably be dissatisfied by the output of replies written from Pentecostal viewpoints. He does, however, remain frustrated by the quality of this output:

> I am somewhat disappointed that the debate which my *Baptism* book seems to have occasioned has not revealed more inadequacies of my thesis than it has . . . I offer such insights as I have received in full expectation that in any discussion or debate they occasion, these insights will be qualified, sharpened, corrected, supplemented, etc. by that discussion and debate. And, as a result, which is what I hope for, my own perception of the issue will be clarified and deepened in the process. Here, however, the necessary qualification seems to be modest, and the main thrust of the thesis of *Baptism* seems to retain its validity.[20]

18. Ibid., 4.

19. With this constituency, "the thesis has been received more like a lead balloon" (Dunn, "Baptism Yet Once More," 4).

20. Dunn, "Baptism Again," 43.

This book will review the responses to which Dunn refers and consider from another viewpoint (my own Pentecostal one) whether Dunn's
position has been successfully challenged and countered. Is Dunn right
to rue the paucity of "inadequacies" that Pentecostals have found in his
thesis? And, even if inadequacies have been unearthed, has a justifiable
alternative been espoused? These are the questions that will occupy the
attention of the next two chapters.

However, before the content of the debate is reviewed in detail,
two things are needed. The first is, for those who have never read
Dunn's *Baptism* or who have not done so for decades, to summarize
the findings of his research as they relate to Luke's two-volume history
of Christian beginnings. The other thing required is an introductory
word about the course and dynamics of the debate, and I will come to
that later in this chapter. First, we turn to the method and contents of
Dunn's doctoral studies.

DUNN'S *BAPTISM*

The first part of Dunn's book is a study of the Gospels. This begins not
with passages, but with historical events: particularly the preaching of
John the Baptist and Jesus' anointing at the Jordan River. From the event,
Dunn expands to consider the evangelists' interpretations, noting any
distinctions between the accounts. This inevitably leads him to consider
source-critical and redactional issues. It also means that his remarks
about Luke's pneumatology are dispersed among his studies of the other
Gospel writers. Nevertheless, his view of the Lukan understanding can
be gleaned with relative ease.

In his study of Acts, however, Dunn adopts the method that will
serve him for his later studies of the Epistles. He identifies each conversion-initiation context and studies each one, passage by passage. His
exegesis is chiefly lexical and syntactical. He does not concern himself
overtly with redactional issues, such as the handling by Luke or his
sources of Joel 2:28–32 at Acts 2:17–21. Neither does he discuss nar-
ratological issues. Another significant difference between Dunn and
some of his respondents is that he does not have an early chapter that
surveys ideas about the Spirit held within early Judaism. None of these
methodological gaps weakens his case, however. What Dunn may lack in
discussion of background or in breadth of exegetical method, he more

than makes up for with simple exegetical care. So to the findings of this exegesis we now turn.

The Anointing of Jesus

Dunn's understanding of Luke's pneumatology begins to emerge in his third chapter, "The Experience of Jesus at Jordan." Dunn first points out the superficial plausibility of Pentecostal interpretations of the experience: Christ's experience of the Spirit is a simple paradigm of a subsequent anointing in a Christian life. Luke declared that John the Baptist was filled with the Holy Spirit from birth, and so he very probably understood that Jesus was as well, for Jesus was conceived by the Spirit (Luke 1:35), increasingly filled with wisdom and grace (Luke 2:40, 52), and aware of his divine sonship (Luke 2:49). His anointing might therefore truly be seen as a *second* experience of the Spirit. Furthermore, this anointing was clearly an equipping for future ministry and could rightly be called a baptism in the Spirit.

However, Dunn considers that the greatest weakness of this Pentecostal view is in what it fails to recognize. The anointing beside the Jordan was not, in Luke's eyes, merely something that happened to Jesus. It was the pivotal introduction of a new epoch in salvation history. It was the beginning of the messianic era. Thus while it "may possibly be described as a second experience of the Spirit for Jesus, it was not a second experience of the new covenant."[21]

Dunn's evidence for this claim is first the difference between the future-orientated preaching of John the Baptist ("It's coming!") and the fulfillment-orientated declarations of Jesus himself ("It's come!"). Secondly, the Jordan narrative contains clear eschatological features: the open heaven, the dove, and the heavenly voice. Thirdly, the Jordan event is portrayed as Jesus' entry into a new role, brought on by the new age: the role of representing Israel as the new Adam. Luke portrayed this role not just by paralleling Matthew's depiction of Christ tested in the wilderness for forty days, but even before this by providing Jesus' genealogy back to Adam himself.

So the Jordan experience may be a powerful anointing, but is primarily, even essentially, initiatory. It "initiated the End-time and initiated

---

21. Dunn, *Baptism*, 24–25.

Jesus into it."[22] As such, it is paradigmatic not of a subsequent Christian experience, but of conversion-initiation itself, for it is this conversion that initiates a follower of Jesus into the new covenant.

The Day of Pentecost

Dunn's view of Pentecost as it was presented by Luke is very similar to his view of Christ's anointing: it *was* an empowering, but it was *primarily* initiatory. This is because Pentecost marked the opening of the next epoch in Luke's three-fold salvation history: the age of the church, which was the age of the Spirit. Until Pentecost, only Christ could receive the Spirit, for the sin of all others was not yet purged by his baptism of fire. But Pentecost was a "watershed in salvation-history, the beginning of the new age and new covenant, not for Jesus this time, but now for His disciples."[23]

How did Luke make this clear, according to Dunn?

a. Pentecost, and not the cross, was the climax of the "Christ-epoch" of salvation-history.

b. Pentecost was a new beginning. Not only did its record form the start of a new book, but the event ushered in a new age. The election of Matthias by casting lots (Acts 1:26) was deliberately included beforehand to illustrate life without the Spirit's activity. But now, and only now, Christ received the Spirit to give (Acts 2:33) and the subsequent outpouring fulfilled Joel's prophecy of the "last days": the "distinctively Christian dispensation."[24]

c. Pentecost was the arrival of the new covenant. The "promise" of Acts 1:4; 2:33, 39 recalls the Abrahamic covenant (Dunn invites us to compare Acts 7:17; 13:23; 26:6), for Acts 2:39 ("The promise is to you, and your children, and to all those far off . . .") mirrors Genesis 17:7–10 (The covenant is for "you and your seed after you for generations"). Furthermore, by the time Luke wrote, Pentecost was celebrated to commemorate Sinai. So "the thought of Pentecost as the giving of the new Torah . . .

---

22. Ibid., 31.
23. Ibid., 40.
24. Ibid., 47.

indicates that for Luke Pentecost was the beginning of the new covenant . . . and that the Spirit is the essence of the new covenant."[25]

d. Pentecost inaugurated the church. Christ's followers could only confess him as Lord (Acts 2:36) once assured of his exaltation to lordship by the gift of the Spirit. This confession was foundational to the church's existence. Also, the church's characteristic activities only now emerged (Acts 2:42). As the church was not born until this time, and since by definition all Christians belong to the church, "there were no Christians (properly speaking) prior to Pentecost."[26]

e. Pentecost was the inception of faith. In Acts 11:17, "Peter tells us . . . that the spiritual state of the 120 prior to Pentecost was precisely that of Cornelius prior to his reception of the Spirit."[27]

In conclusion to his chapter about Pentecost, Dunn warns that the life of the 120 prior to Pentecost cannot be used as a paradigm for the experience of today's new believer, precisely because that life was pre-Christian. Pentecost is itself a paradigm not of a second blessing, but of becoming a Christian.[28]

The Samaritan Reception

Next Dunn tackles Acts 8:4–25, with its "riddle": despite the belief and baptism in water of the Samaritan converts, they did not receive the Spirit until some time had elapsed. Seeking to solve this riddle, Dunn presents evidence that Luke was deliberately portraying the initial Samaritan response as defective.

a. The superstitious Samaritans responded to Simon the Sorcerer without deep discernment. Luke used the same verb *prosechō* ("pay attention to") of their response to both Simon and Philip, indicating a reaction to Philip's message and miracles of similar undiscerning superficiality. Its origin, as the word

---

25. Ibid., 49.
26. Ibid., 51.
27. Ibid., 51.
28. Ibid., 53.

homothumadon ("with one accord") in Acts 8:6 indicates, was "the herd-instinct of a popular mass-movement."[29]

b. The Samaritans believed *tō Philippō* ("Philip", in the dative), not *epi ton Kurion* ("in the Lord"). This use of the dative with *pisteuein* ("believe") signifies mere intellectual assent, Dunn asserts.

c. Simon's belief and baptism were shallow and unreforming (Acts 8:9, 13, 18–24), and Luke was clear that his "faith and baptism were precisely like those of the other Samaritans."[30]

d. Because in New Testament times reception of the Spirit was the evidence that someone was a Christian, it follows that "Luke's aim is to highlight the difference between true and false Christianity."[31]

Dunn's conclusion about Luke's presentation follows naturally: the Samaritans were not Christians until they received the Spirit. Once carefully exegeted, this vital passage offers no support to Pentecostalism after all.

Paul's Conversion

Luke's account of Paul's conversion is, writes Dunn, another key passage for Pentecostalism. Paul is viewed as being converted on the Damascus road, for he addressed Jesus as "Lord," and was himself subsequently addressed by Ananias as "brother." Only after three days was he filled with the Spirit (Acts 9:3–5, 9, 17).

Dunn argues that this view misunderstands Luke.

a. Paul's *kurie* (Acts 9:5; usually "Lord") means no more here than "sir" (as it does in Acts 10:4 and 16:30).

b. Ananias' "Brother" (Acts 9:17) possibly means "fellow Jew," and was simply used to put Paul at his ease.

c. Ananias viewed Paul, when he met him, as someone who still required to have his sins washed away (Acts 22:16).

29. Ibid., 65.
30. Ibid., 66.
31. Ibid., 66.

d. Paul, testifying much later at his trials, did not distinguish between what God had said on the Damascus road (Acts 26:16–18) and what God said through Ananias (Acts 22:14–15). So his conversion must be regarded as a process lasting for the three days.

e. Paul's blindness remained for those three days. This is hardly symbolic of completed conversion (!), but rather symbolic, for Luke, of turmoil and of crushing conviction. It was his new sight that displayed his new life, mediated through his reception of the Spirit.

In conclusion, Luke portrayed not Paul's second blessing, but his three-day conversion: "The experience of being filled with the Spirit was as much an integral part of his conversion as his meeting with Jesus."[32]

Cornelius' Conversion

This account places the Pentecostal "in difficulty from the start."[33] While some Pentecostals argue that Cornelius was regenerate prior to Peter's sermon (which, Dunn notes, was not Luke's understanding—Acts 11:14, 18), others perceive that he was saved *during* the sermon, viewing his Spirit baptism as a closely succeeding, or simultaneous but distinct, event. These views, argues Dunn, do not fit the evidence. The Spirit fell when Peter was speaking about faith and forgiveness, not about baptism in the Spirit (Acts 10:43–44). Thus at the moment Cornelius trusted God for forgiveness, he actually received the Spirit, "not instead of the promised forgiveness but as the bearer of it."[34] The synonymy within Acts 15:8–9 (Dunn also notes Acts 11:14–18) confirms this: "God's giving of the Holy Spirit is equivalent to his cleansing of their hearts."[35] Dunn's understanding of Luke is unequivocal: "the baptism in the Spirit *is* God's act of acceptance, of forgiveness, cleansing and salvation."[36]

---

32. Ibid., 77–78.
33. Ibid., 79.
34. Ibid., 80.
35. Ibid., 81–82.
36. Ibid., 82; italics added.

The Ephesian Outpouring

In his next chapter, Dunn studies Acts 19:1–7, an important passage for Pentecostals. They come to any or all of three conclusions: the Ephesians were Christian before meeting Paul; Paul's question implies that a Christian could be without the Spirit; time elapsed between the Ephesians' receiving baptism and their receiving the Spirit.

Dunn understands Luke's words differently. Luke did not present these Ephesians as Christians. They were ignorant about the Spirit and about Jesus. They yet required Christian baptism in water. They were called *tinas mathētas* ("some disciples"). Luke's formula for Christians was *hoi mathētai* ("*the* disciples"). This unique use of *mathētai* ("disciples") without the article ("the") distanced the group from *the* disciples in Ephesus. Paul's first question ("Did you receive the Holy Spirit when you believed?"), with its *pisteusantes* ("believing"; "when you believed"), was one of "suspicion and surprise." Paul asked, "Did you receive the *Holy Spirit* when you believed?"[37]—as if his query were, in effect, "What 'spirit' did you receive?" His second question ("Into what then were you baptized?") clarifies the connection in Paul's mind between baptism into Christ and baptism in the Spirit. Furthermore, their second answer ("Into the baptism of John") confirmed his suspicions: they were not Christians. Any time interval that Pentecostals might claim between baptism and the laying on of hands is fictional. The latter is the climax of the former: "the one action leads into and reaches its conclusion in the other with no discernible break."[38] In conclusion, Dunn understands Luke to have portrayed just one act of the Spirit in the Ephesians' lives: that baptism in the Spirit whereby they became Christians.

Baptism: Dunn's Conclusions

For Dunn, the evidence has all pointed one way: Luke's pneumatology does not support Pentecostalism's key distinctive: its doctrine of subsequence. Reception of the Holy Spirit, while being an overwhelming experiential empowering, was initiatory in character, bringing the recipient into the new covenant. Jesus' anointing at the Jordan River and the outpouring on the day of Pentecost were essentially unique, for each represented the dawning of a new era: the age of the new covenant, first

37. Ibid., 86; italics original.
38. Ibid., 87.

for Jesus and then for his followers. However, as archetypes of all future Christian experience, they represent not a second blessing, but Christian conversion itself. Luke's picture is only confirmed by all subsequent conversions he described. Baptism in the Holy Spirit is not merely necessarily and automatically co-incident with the cleansing of salvation: "these two are one—two ways of describing the same thing." "Baptism in the Spirit is God's act of . . . salvation."[39]

While reaching this conclusion about Luke's writings, Dunn also reaches precisely the same conclusion about the rest of the New Testament. Thus he sees a highly consistent picture emerging from the writings of the various authors. There is no dichotomy, for instance, between Luke and Paul. In the views of these and the other New Testament writers, a single overall pneumatology is presented, which includes the teaching that only through reception of the Spirit does someone become a Christian.

DUNN'S LATER CONTRIBUTIONS

Since publishing *Baptism*, Dunn has written three articles that directly and overtly engage with his Pentecostal debaters, as well as various other books, such as *Jesus and the Spirit* and a commentary on Acts, that engage in part with the debate. The first of the three articles, "Baptism in the Spirit: A Response to Pentecostal Scholarship on Luke-Acts," was published in *JPT* in 1993. The second, published in *JEPTA* in 1998, was called "Baptism in the Holy Spirit . . . Yet Once More." The third, published again in *JPT*, appeared in 2010 under the title, "Baptism in the Holy Spirit . . . Yet Once More—Again." Not only are these titles, with their repetition of "Baptism in the (Holy) Spirit," potentially confusing, but also the later titles might lead us to believe that Dunn has become increasingly bored by the subject and would wish that his various respondents might concentrate on other subject areas in their debates with him. However, such an impression would be far from accurate. He writes in his 1998 article of the Holy Spirit being, in terms of New Testament study, his "first love."[40] In 2010, he still writes of finding Paul's contribution to New Testament pneumatology "fascinating."[41] And the content of

39. Ibid., 82.
40. Dunn, "Baptism Yet Once More," 3.
41. Dunn, "Baptism Again," 36.

the articles continues to evidence a lively interest in the subjects under discussion. In the following paragraphs I will draw out from the articles any observations Dunn makes about Luke-Acts and its pneumatology that add to what he has covered in his book on the subject.

In his 1993 article, Dunn responds to the first wave of Pentecostal criticism of his original thesis. As will emerge later in this book, a particular methodological criticism made by more than one Pentecostal is that Dunn unduly homogenizes the breadth of view expressed by the different New Testament writers: he treats Luke and Paul, for instance, as if they had the same pneumatology—and that pneumatology is Paul's! Dunn makes a couple of interesting observations here. One is that, "To criticise me . . . for reading Luke-Acts with Pauline spectacles, is, of course, to acknowledge that my findings are sound so far as Paul was concerned."[42] Of course, my book is mainly about Luke-Acts, but chapter 4 will briefly broaden out beyond Luke's writing to consider Paul's, and will return then to the question of how Pentecostals regard Dunn's exegesis of Paul's letters, for it is an important aspect of the whole discussion. A related observation offered by Dunn at this time is his admission that "it is only proper for me to acknowledge that my conclusions in *Baptism in the* [sic] *Spirit* are clearest in Paul and John."[43] However, if a reader at the time regarded that admission as the first "chink of light" that would lead to Dunn's backing down concerning his reading of Luke-Acts, that was certainly not to be the case. Dunn remains as forthright as ever concerning his overall conclusions.

Dunn is also careful to reaffirm his agreement with Pentecostalism that Spirit reception as portrayed by Luke is charismatic in nature.[44] This is an important emphasis, for it will emerge that some Pentecostal critiques view Dunn as in effect anti-charismatic as well as "anti-Pentecostal." This is far from true.

In his 1998 article, Dunn pays greater attention to concepts lying behind the New Testament writings than he does in his book. In a section that asks, "Is There a Primary Conceptuality for the Spirit?" he concludes from his study of the Old Testament and relevant Jewish writings that the answer is affirmative. Even though in the thinking about the Spirit on

42. Dunn, "Baptism: A Response," 224.

43. Ibid. Also ibid., 242: "the soteriological function of the Spirit is much more prominent in Paul than in Luke."

44. Ibid., 226–27, 241.

which Luke must have drawn there is a "spectrum of usage where different meanings run into each other and different conceptualities merge with one another," there is nevertheless a discernible center to these concepts: there is only one Spirit, who is "the self-manifestation of God in powerful activity." In relation to humanity, "the primary conceptualisation of the *ruach* [the Hebrew for 'wind,' 'breath,' or 'S/spirit'] is as the breath of life, as the life-force, as divinely breathed and sustained vitality."[45] This unity of concept—the Spirit granting life—in Luke's background makes Dunn suspicious of any portrayal of New Testament pneumatology that sharply distinguishes between the views of, say, different authors in the canon. It also causes him to regard it as "scarcely credible" that "Luke does not think of the Spirit as life-giving."[46] Whether Dunn has accurately reflected Luke's conceptual background, and whether he has then imposed his view of that background on what Luke actually writes, will be matters that will naturally emerge later in this book.

At this stage, there is but one further brief comment to be made about Dunn's view of Lukan pneumatology from his 1998 article, and it concerns Peter's Pentecost sermon. In a way that Dunn did not do in his book, he now notes that Luke extends the quotation of Joel's prophecy (Acts 2:17–21) all the way through to Joel 2:32a, which speaks of salvation for all those who call on the Lord. Luke then "repeats the echo of Joel 2:32 at the end of Peter's speech" (referring to Acts 2:39). Thereby, "Luke deliberately brackets the significance of Pentecost with the complete Joel quotation, and thus highlights the significance of the Spirit as both an inspiring power and a saving power."[47] Dunn's handling of Pentecost will gain fuller attention later, but for now it will suffice to observe that if Luke were deliberately seeking to echo Joel in his quotation of Peter in Acts 2:39 ("The promise is for . . . all whom the Lord our God will call"), he would have extended the quotation not merely to Joel 2:32a, but to the end of Joel 2:32 (" . . . whom the LORD calls/has called"). This is a closer parallel than the one Dunn identifies at the start of Joel 2:32, which reads, "everyone who calls on the name of the LORD."

In his 2010 article Dunn responds, with respect to Luke-Acts, to an article written by Roger Stronstad. This does not lead Dunn to offer

45. Dunn, "Baptism Yet Once More," 8.

46. Ibid., 9, 17.

47. Ibid., 17. Dunn makes the same point more briefly in "Baptism: A Response," 237.

much new material, but there is a little that is worthy of note here. In particular, he has now slightly altered his characterization of the Samaritan reception, recorded in Acts 8:4–24. In his 1970 book, as noted earlier in this chapter, he regarded Philip's ministry as ineffective: when the apostles Peter and John arrived from Jerusalem, they found credulous attenders to Philip and his miracles, not believing disciples of Jesus. In 1979, replying to one of his critics, Dunn did have to acknowledge of the Samaritan episode that, "this was not the strongest part of my discussion of Acts."[48] Yet he continued to defend his position staunchly. By 1996 he was allowing doubt, and considering two possibilities: "Whether the rationale is that the Samaritans' faith fell short of full commitment to the Lord (8:12), or that baptism even 'in the name of the Lord Jesus' was in itself not enough."[49] In 2010, however, he can write simply of the "effectiveness of Philip's ministry," and admit that his attempt in *Baptism* to explain the Samaritan "riddle" "may not be very successful, and need not be given much weight."[50] However, he does not seem to concede what a "foothold" for other readings of Acts he is allowing once he acknowledges any inadequacy in his reading of this passage. This is true, however unusual the situation might have been or appeared and however urgent the remedial action of Peter and John must have been.

THE DEBATE AND DEBATERS

As I mentioned earlier in the chapter, a special session of the Society of Biblical Literature conference in New Orleans in November 2009 was devoted to Dunn's *Baptism* and its repercussions. One of the contributors to that symposium, and therefore to the series of articles published in *JPT* 19, is the Pentecostal scholar Roger Stronstad, and it is with his reflections that I will begin my study of the debate. He considers the impact of Dunn's *Baptism* on Pentecostalism and offers two suggestions concerning its extent: in one respect, he claims, Dunn's work had no effect on Pentecostalism; on the other hand, "Dunn's challenge forced Pentecostals to articulate a more sophisticated interpretation of Luke's data about the 'Baptism in the Holy Spirit.'"[51] By his first suggestion,

---

48. Dunn, "They Believed Philip Preaching," 216.

49. Dunn, *Acts*, 111.

50. Dunn, "Baptism Again," 34 and n. 6.

51. Stronstad, "Forty Years On," 6.

Stronstad no doubt means that we Pentecostals remain as convinced as ever by our doctrine of subsequence, despite Dunn's best efforts to convince us to the contrary. This may well be true of the great majority of Pentecostals, but Dunn has had at least one (highly prominent) convert: Max Turner.[52] When Turner first read Dunn's book back in 1970, he found himself exclaiming, "Dunn is *wrong* on Luke."[53] It was Dunn's work, and Turner's disagreement with Dunn's position, that led to Turner's choice of doctoral research.[54] At this stage, as Turner researched his "Luke and the Spirit," he was "a young and enthusiastically Pentecostal student."[55] The extent to which his views altered, if at all, prior to 1980 (the date his doctoral work was submitted to the University of Cambridge) is unclear. However, as he acknowledges,[56] and Dunn notes,[57] his position has altered over the years, as he has continued to engage in the debate stimulated by Dunn's work. His evolving positions are recorded in his writing. Distinctions are discernible between his 1980 doctoral thesis, "Luke and the Spirit," and his more recent major contributions, *Power from on High* and *The Holy Spirit and Spiritual Gifts*, both published in 1996.

I mention Turner particularly at this stage because while he is only one of several debaters with Dunn whose work I shall review, he stands out as someone who has changed his view *and admitted it*. He is also one of the most thorough Lukan pneumatologists among those I discuss. For these twin reasons, my engagement with his views will take up what might otherwise look like an undue proportion of my attention.

Turning now to Stronstad's second suggestion concerning Dunn's impact (in short, that Dunn encouraged us Pentecostals to think),

52. Frank Macchia implies that Gordon Fee has also been influenced by Dunn in developing his view of Spirit baptism (Macchia, *Baptized in the Spirit*, 68). Note too how Mittelstadt places Fee first in his list of Pentecostal responses to Dunn's *Baptism*, while admitting that Fee has not actually responded to Dunn as such. The implication is that Mittelstadt suspects at least some influence by Dunn on Fee in this area of doctrine (Mittelstadt, *Reading Luke-Acts*, 49–50). Everts records that she converted the other way: "I reread Dunn and became a Pentecostal" (Everts, "Pauline Letters," 18).

53. Turner, "James Dunn's *Baptism*," 25; italics his.

54. Turner, *Power from on High*, 11; Turner, "Luke and the Spirit," 27–28: "The questions he [Dunn] has raised are those which stimulated this research, and much of this study may be considered as a critique of Dunn's widely accepted hypothesis."

55. Turner, *Power from on High*, 11; cf. Turner, "James Dunn's *Baptism*," 25.

56. Turner, *Power from on High*, 11; Turner, "James Dunn's *Baptism*," 30.

57. Dunn, "Baptism Again," 42: "Our paths which initially had seemed to diverge quite markedly now seemed to be coming closer and closer."

Stronstad is undoubtedly right, as is attested by the very debate that this book reviews. In the earlier decades of the twentieth century, sadly, Pentecostals were not generally well known for their depth of thinking, however profound their personal experience and however dramatic their Christian commitment. For instance, Smith Wigglesworth may have spoken for many early Pentecostals when he declared, "Faith cometh by hearing, and hearing by the Word of God—not by reading commentaries!"[58] Relatively unthinking Bible reading has been criticized from without[59] and from within: Gordon Fee has written of his fellow Pentecostals, "their attitude towards Scripture regularly has included a general disregard for scientific exegesis and carefully thought-out hermeneutics . . . In place of scientific hermeneutics there developed a kind of pragmatic hermeneutics—obey what should be taken literally; spiritualize, allegorize or devotionalize the rest."[60]

This phenomenon was perhaps widely present among earlier Pentecostals for the reason that Pentecostal church leaders had not traditionally had the access to academic teaching that was available or sought in other denominations.[61] But in the later decades of the twentieth century, this situation was beginning to change fast—and Stronstad was one of the pioneers: he represented Pentecostals who retained their doctrinal and practical distinctives while engaging with other viewpoints through the rigors of academic research and writing. In fact, Stronstad's first relevant book was hailed by Clark Pinnock in the following words:

> I am quite frankly excited at the appearance of Roger Stronstad's book *The Charismatic Theology of St. Luke*. Until now people have had to recognize Pentecostalism as a powerful force in the areas of spirituality, church growth, and world mission, but they have not felt it had much to offer for biblical, theological and intellectual foundations. But this is fast changing, and with the appearance of this book we may be seeing the first motions of a wave of intellectually convincing Pentecostal theology, which will sweep

---

58. Quoted by Frodsham, *Smith Wigglesworth: Apostle of Faith*, 73.

59. E.g., MacArthur, *Charismatic Chaos*, ch. 4.

60. Fee, *Gospel and Spirit*, 85–86; similarly, Fee, "Why Pentecostals Read Their Bibles Poorly."

61. Anderson, *Introduction to Pentecostalism*, 243. For discussion of more recent changes in Pentecostal attitudes to education, see Anderson, "Pentecostals and Academic Theology," ch. 13.

in upon us in the next decades. Watch out you evangelicals—the young Pentecostal scholars are coming![62]

The benefit of some decades of hindsight allows us to judge that Pinnock was right. Furthermore, at least as regards thinking about baptism in the Spirit, Dunn's work has been real "grist to the mill" of this Pentecostal development. The extent to which Dunn's *Baptism* specifically has contributed to this keener Pentecostal thinking is significant,[63] and for that we Pentecostals all owe Dunn a great debt of gratitude.

Given Dunn's disappointed comments offered in 2010 and quoted a few paragraphs ago, it seems that Dunn himself may have wanted to encourage this development of Pentecostal thought. It is certainly the case that, back in 1970, he did not view every aspect of Pentecostalism with disdain: far from it. In his preface to *Baptism*, he wrote:

> It will become evident that this doctrine [of baptism in the Holy Spirit] cannot escape heavy criticism from a New Testament standpoint, but I would hope also that the importance and value of the Pentecostal emphasis will not be lost sight of or ignored. In particular, the Pentecostal contribution should cause Christians in the "main-line" denominations to look afresh with critical eyes at the place they give to the Holy Spirit in doctrine and experience and in their various theologies of conversion, initiation, and baptism. And any voice which bids us test familiar traditions by the yardstick of the New Testament is to be welcomed.[64]

This is praise indeed from the pen of one who regarded and regards Pentecostalism as resting on such shaky exegetical foundations! However, this reference to Dunn's praise of Pentecostalism is, of course, not to suggest that his kind words extend to Pentecostals' understanding of key passages. Dunn can happily write of New Testament passages being "a crushing rejoinder to Pentecostal ideas," or knocking "the Pentecostals' case on the head," or cutting "the ground away from under the Pentecostal."[65] No wonder Pentecostals reacted!

Over the years since its publication, then, Dunn's book has evoked a considerable Pentecostal response. It is easy to imagine that any

62. Clark Pinnock, "Foreword," in Stronstad, *Charismatic Theology*, vii.

63. The significance has been noted recently in Mittelstadt, *Reading Luke-Acts*, ch. 2, which he titles, "The Dunn Factor."

64. Dunn, *Baptism*, viii.

65. Ibid., 107, 123, 135.

Pentecostals worth their salt writing at an academic level about Lukan pneumatology can hardly avoid making at least some reference to Dunn's work. Where it is appropriate, I will refer to their views as the book proceeds. However, in order to gain a due sense of focus and progression, I am going to concentrate particularly on those works that engage explicitly and protractedly with Dunn—and particularly with what Dunn states about Luke-Acts. This will mean reviewing six such responses, offered by the following authors, whom I will list in the chronological order of their first relevant work (either publication or academic submission).

Roger Stronstad

Stronstad is a Canadian Pentecostal, working as Associate Professor in Bible and Theology at Summit Pacific College, Abbotsford, British Columbia. Stronstad's *The Charismatic Theology of St. Luke*, though published in 1984, represents the earliest response to Dunn in this review, being originally submitted as a Master's thesis to Regent College in 1975.[66] Stronstad's book is neither overtly nor solely a response to Dunn. Nevertheless, such a response is a marked feature of its contents. While both Pinnock's foreword and the opening paragraph of Stronstad's own text might suggest to the reader that the book will reply equally to "two benchmark books . . . *A Theology of the Holy Spirit* by Frederick Dale Bruner and *Baptism in the Holy Spirit* by James D. G. Dunn,"[67] the former "benchmark book" is not referred to again by Stronstad, while Dunn's work is mentioned repeatedly, with more of Stronstad's end-notes referring to *Baptism in the Holy Spirit* than to any other book. He has since written *The Prophethood of All Believers*, which as its subtitle implies (*A Study in Luke's Charismatic Theology*) continues the theme of his earlier work, and *Baptized and Filled with the Holy Spirit*. However, they only refer minimally to Dunn.

Max Turner

Turner is Professor of New Testament Studies at the London School of Theology. His "Luke and the Spirit" was submitted to the University of Cambridge for a PhD in 1980. As I mentioned earlier, Turner reacted negatively to what Dunn had written in his *Baptism* about Luke, and this

---

66. Stronstad, *Charismatic Theology*, v.

67. Ibid., 1.

disagreement affected the choice and the content of Turner's doctoral research. It was not published in full, although some of its content was published in various journal articles over the next few years. His *Power from on High* and *The Holy Spirit and Spiritual Gifts* both came out in 1996. Of the two, *Power from on High* contains by far the greater detail on Luke-Acts, as is attested by its subtitle: *The Spirit in Israel's Restoration and Witness in Luke-Acts*. It is not merely an updating of his doctoral work. It is that, in the sense that it includes much of the latter's content while taking note of subsequent scholarship. But as I noted earlier, it also indicates some degree of change in Turner's viewpoint from his 1980 position, and this adds particular interest to his contribution.

Howard Ervin

The late Howard Ervin (1915–2009) was a Professor of Old Testament at Oral Roberts University. Denominationally a Baptist, he experienced a "personal Pentecost" in about 1962, as someone who already had a significant theological education and a doctorate in theology.[68] After being baptized in the Spirit, he wrote *These Are Not Drunken, As Ye Suppose*, which was published in 1968. This was one of the first stoutly theological defenses of Pentecostal doctrine.

But the appearance in 1970 of Dunn's work called for a further contribution. Ervin's response to Dunn, *Conversion-Initiation and the Baptism in the Holy Spirit*, was, like Stronstad's *Charismatic Theology*, published in 1984. It is the most overt and direct reply of those under review, as the wording of the subtitle makes clear: *An Engaging Critique of James D. G. Dunn's Baptism in the Holy Spirit*. He has also since rewritten *These Are Not Drunken, As Ye Suppose* under the title *Spirit-Baptism: A Biblical Investigation*, published in 1987, but in that work he makes little reference to Dunn.

David Petts

Petts was until his retirement the Principal of Mattersey Hall, the training College of the British Assemblies of God. His unpublished MTh thesis was titled, "The Baptism in the Holy Spirit in Relation to Christian Initiation." This was submitted to The University of Nottingham in

---

68. Justus du Plessis, "Foreword" in Ervin, *Spirit-Baptism*, xi.

1987.[69] The second half of his work, titled "An Examination of Key NT Passages," is a discussion of, in particular, "the now classic contribution of James Dunn along with Howard Ervin's recent critique of Dunn's work."[70] Dunn's *Baptism* is referred to constantly throughout this half of the dissertation and largely dictates the content of Petts' work.

James Shelton

Shelton is a Professor of New Testament and Early Christian Literature at Oral Roberts University. He gained his PhD at the University of Stirling, and his work was published in 1991 under the title *Mighty in Word and Deed: The Role of the Holy Spirit in Luke-Acts*. Shelton's book contains perhaps the least direct response to Dunn's thinking of those reviewed here. Nonetheless, his eleventh chapter, "The Holy Spirit and Believers in Acts," and an appendix, "Jesus, John, the Spirit, and the New Age," contain sufficient interaction to merit a brief section in this book.

Robert Menzies

Menzies is an American Pentecostal missionary, currently working in Asia. He has two books published on this topic: *The Development of Early Christian Pneumatology with Special Reference to Luke-Acts* (1991) and *Empowered for Witness: The Spirit in Luke-Acts* (1994). In practice, the overlap between these works is so great that the latter can be considered as a republishing of the former. Menzies' *Development* was originally a doctoral dissertation presented to the University of Aberdeen in 1989. As its name implies, it is, like Stronstad's book, far more than just a response to Dunn. Nonetheless, a perusal of the text and footnotes of the thesis reveals the degree to which it interacts with him.

CONCLUSIONS

In summary, this chapter has introduced us to the topic of the book—the Pentecostal doctrine of baptism in the Holy Spirit—and shown that an excellent way to study this doctrine is to review a debate that was started by James Dunn in 1970. We have seen the centrality of Spirit baptism as a doctrine to Pentecostalism, and the centrality of

---

69. Dunn was Petts' external examiner for this dissertation (email message from Petts to author, July 7, 2010).

70. Petts, "Baptism in the Holy Spirit," 43.

Luke-Acts in biblical studies supporting this doctrine. We have also noted the great importance of Dunn's part in the debate surrounding the doctrine. Finally, we have "met" the Pentecostals who sit around the debating table facing Dunn.

Now that I have introduced these themes and these people, I will in the next chapter focus on the Pentecostal respondents to Dunn and set out their critiques of Dunn's work. Again I will do this in chronological order of first relevant publication or academic submission. Then chapter 3 will consider the strengths and weaknesses of the various alternatives to Dunn's position that they have put forward over the years that the debate has lasted. In chapter 4, I will discuss what the findings of the book thus far imply for a view of being "baptized with the Holy Spirit" that listens to other key New Testament scriptures, not just to Luke-Acts. In chapter 5, after a summary and concluding development of the findings of previous chapters, I will consider some practical implications that arise for Pentecostalism today.

2

Pentecostal Criticisms of Dunn

INTRODUCTION

M Y LAST CHAPTER INTRODUCED the debate that was sparked by the publication, four decades ago, of Dunn's *Baptism in the Holy Spirit*, and then considered Dunn's work and how his book initiated the debate, before briefly surveying Dunn's more recent contributions to the ongoing discussions. I then introduced the main Pentecostal (and, in the case of Turner, ex-Pentecostal) debaters with Dunn. This chapter now turns to the contributions made by these discussion partners. I will consider their contributions author by author, in the chronological order of their main works. In the case of Turner, he will have two "entries" in this chapter, for his 1996 position is somewhat different from that in 1980.

ROGER STRONSTAD

Stronstad's book *The Charismatic Theology of St. Luke* was a great achievement. It was "the first work by a classical Pentecostal to be taken seriously by non-Pentecostal Lukan scholars."[1] In it, Stronstad set out to tackle what in his opinion was a "silencing" of Luke's pneumatology by many contemporary interpreters. Stronstad asserted that this silencing had been achieved through a denial of three important aspects of Luke's writing. These are that Luke-Acts is theologically homogeneous (for instance, what is meant by "being filled with the Spirit" means the same in Acts as it does in the Gospel); that Luke is an accomplished theologian as well as a skilled historian; and that Luke is an independent theologian whose pneumatology must not be read as if it were John's or Paul's. Stronstad devotes his first chapter to defending these three char-

---

1. Mittelstadt, *Reading Luke-Acts*, 51.

acteristics of Luke's writing. Then, having surveyed the Lukan corpus in his intervening chapters, Stronstad concludes the book by summarizing his view that Luke always presents the Spirit's work in someone's life as vocational, and specifically charismatic and prophetic, rather than as soteriological. In general terms at least, Jesus' anointing with the Spirit, presented early in the Gospel as an equipping for service, is parallel to the disciples' baptism with the Spirit, presented early in Acts as an equipping for service.[2] As I mentioned in chapter 1, Stronstad's work, while by no means merely a response to Dunn's *Baptism*, interacts significantly with Dunn's views. That this is the case is evidenced, among other ways, by the terminology of Stronstad's final sentence of the book before his two-page section of "contemporary application." He writes, "Only those who resist the evidence can continue to interpret the gift of the Holy Spirit in Luke-Acts to be an initiation-conversion experience."[3] Dunn coined the term "conversion-initiation."[4] It has been used by many authors since, but Stronstad's early use of the term, despite his reversal of its elements, suggests that he was implicitly referring to Dunn as the chief "culprit" in his final "denouncement of the opposition."

We turn now to Stronstad's specific criticisms of Dunn's work. Stronstad believes that Dunn has misunderstood Luke's pneumatology. This failure has arisen for two reasons: Dunn's interpretation of Luke has been highly colored by his understanding of Paul; and consequently Dunn has misrepresented the meaning of several significant passages.

Stronstad on Luke's "Pauline" Pneumatology

Dunn has committed what Stronstad calls "illegitimate identity transfer": "Luke's data on the Holy Spirit are interpreted as though they were written by Paul."[5] Paul's phrase "baptized in the Holy Spirit" is understood to signify initiation, and this Pauline meaning is read into Luke's use of that and similar terms.[6] The absurdity of this procedure is illustrated, for

2. Stronstad, *Charismatic Theology*, chs 1, 6.

3. Ibid., 82.

4. Dunn, *Baptism*, 7.

5. Stronstad, *Charismatic Theology*, 9. Stronstad borrows the term *illegitimate identity transfer* from Barr's *Semantics of Biblical Language*. Compare Stronstad's diagnosis in Stronstad, "Unity and Diversity," 16, "Dunn conforms Luke's report of the gift of the Spirit . . . to Paul's doctrine."

6. Stronstad, *Charismatic Theology*, 10.

Stronstad, by the simple fact that while Paul used the phrases *baptized in the Spirit* and *filled with the Spirit* only once each, Luke used the former phrase three times and the latter a total of nine times.[7] The result of this transfer of meaning is the effective silencing of Luke's pneumatology. Dunn should have examined Luke's works "with a mind open to the possibility that his perspective on the Holy Spirit may, in fact, differ from Paul's."[8] Thus a broader database would have been available from which to glean a New Testament pneumatology.

Is Stronstad's criticism accurate? Certainly his is not a lone voice. Turner is as forthright, as we shall see in the next section.[9] Whether Dunn *implicitly* imports Pauline thought into his study of Luke is a verdict that depends upon full exegesis of Luke's and Paul's works.[10] However, it is notable at this stage that Dunn on occasions *explicitly* prioritizes Pauline pneumatology when investigating Luke. For instance, he writes, "Luke seems to share Paul's equation of . . ." "This is certainly Paul's understanding . . . It is very probable therefore that Luke also saw . . ." "Luke's history at this point demonstrates Paul's doctrine."[11] There is at least a hint in these excerpts that the "Pauline spectacles" are on Dunn's nose.[12]

Stronstad on Dunn's Exegesis

Stronstad explicitly criticizes Dunn's exegesis of the passages describing Pentecost and the Samaritan and Ephesian conversions. Stronstad agrees with Dunn that the Pentecost outpouring mirrors the Jordan anointing.[13]

---

7. Ibid., 11. Stronstad's statistics are slightly misleading, for Luke only used Paul's term *plēroō* ("fill") once. Eight instances in Luke-Acts to which Stronstad alludes are uses of another Greek verb, *pimplēmi* (also meaning "fill").

8. Ibid., 11.

9. So too are Petts and Shelton. Petts implicitly has Dunn in mind when he writes that Pentecostalism's critics regard Paul as doctrinally definitive, interpreting Acts in that light (Petts, "Baptism in the Holy Spirit," 83–85). Compare Shelton, *Mighty in Word and Deed*, 127, 149 n. 11. See also Penney, *Missionary Emphasis*, 71 n. 47; 107; Mittelstadt, *Reading Luke-Acts*, 46–47.

10. Though I will not be discussing Paul's letters in any detail in this book, see my "Pentecostal Responses: Pauline Literature" for a review of how these Pentecostal respondents to Dunn have interacted with his reading of Paul. See also chapter 4 for brief comments.

11. Dunn, *Baptism*, 47, 48, 51. Admittedly, the "therefore" in the second quotation refers to a logical deduction not *only* from Paul's understanding.

12. Dunn refutes the charge to this day (Dunn, "Baptism Again," 33).

13. Stronstad, *Charismatic Theology*, 51–52.

However, he understands the Jordan event differently. His main departure from Dunn in method is to study the "Inauguration Narrative" through to Christ's preaching at Nazareth (Luke 4:16–30), for this is Luke's record of Christ's understanding of what happened at the Jordan River.[14] The fulfillment of Isaiah 61:1–2 shows that the "gift of the Spirit to Jesus . . . is vocational. This vocational gift is specifically prophetic."[15] And so, because it parallels Jordan, Pentecost "has the same primary charismatic meaning for the mission of the disciples."[16] The overemphasis on initiation results, believes Stronstad, from an overemphasis on discontinuity between the epochs of Luke's salvation history. Stronstad observes the tendency of scholars following Conzelmann to divide salvation history as depicted by Luke into three eras: those of Israel, Jesus, and the church. In this understanding Pentecost marks the beginning of the third epoch. Dunn, Stronstad implies, has followed Conzelmann's unjustified division here, and has thereby distorted Luke-Acts.[17]

Stronstad finds Dunn's exegesis of Acts 8:14–19 "contrived." For him, it is a good example of how Dunn's imposition of Pauline categories has damaged his exegesis of Lukan passages. The passage is an equally good example of the distinctiveness of Luke's understanding of Spirit reception, which is here obviously "devoid of any soteriological connotations,"[18] because the Samaritans were already Christians and the Spirit was given to equip them for missionary discipleship. However, Stronstad does not provide any exegetical detail behind his reasons for dismissing Dunn's understanding of the passage.

In his brief study of Acts 19:1–7, Stronstad goes a little further in tackling the exegetical issues. Paul's question to the Ephesian disciples ("Did you receive the Holy Spirit?"—Acts 19:2) was to real Christians, declared Luke. *Tinas mathētas* (Acts 19:1—"some disciples"; "certain disciples") describes the Ephesians as Christians just as much as *tis mathētēs* ("a certain disciple") categorizes Ananias and Timothy as Christians (Acts 9:10; 16:1).[19] Furthermore, the question's "context" is

14. Ibid., 42.

15. Ibid., 45.

16. Ibid., 52.

17. Ibid., 3, 62. Writing in 2010, Dunn plays down the significance of a "three-epoch" reading of Luke-Acts for his position (Dunn, "Baptism Again," 41).

18. Stronstad, *Charismatic Theology*, 63–65, quotations from 64.

19. Ibid., 90 n. 4. Dunn later conceded the relative effectiveness of this argument, but regarded his own point as speculative and peripheral (Dunn, "Baptism: A Response,"

suggested by its "solution": prophecy and tongues. Thus the context was obviously not initiatory, but prophetic.[20] Stronstad's second point, about context, is weak, for surely the solution to the problem highlighted by Paul's questions was as much the Ephesians' (initiating) baptism in water as their (charismatic) reception of the Spirit. However, his first point, about the meaning of *tinas mathētas*, is stronger. However, even that is not conclusive, for in the context of Acts 18:24–25; 19:3, Luke may have understood the Ephesians to be disciples of John the Baptist,[21] or even conceivably disciples of Apollos.

Conclusion

In noting Dunn's adherence to Pauline concepts, Stronstad offers a plausible diagnosis of Dunn's prime weakness in his overall approach to Luke's pneumatology. Also, in his brief survey of Lukan passages, Stronstad has at least cast doubt on some of Dunn's exegetical points. His greatest contribution in this respect has been to highlight Luke 4:16–30 as the passage in which Luke most clearly presents *his* understanding of what happened to Jesus at the Jordan River.

MAX TURNER, 1980

In the 1970s, at roughly the same time that Stronstad in Canada was conducting his Master's research, on the other side of the Atlantic Max Turner was conducting his doctoral research. As mentioned in chapter 1, this was partly in response to Dunn's *Baptism*. While Dunn's more general critique of Pentecostal viewpoints was no doubt of concern to Turner, it was Dunn's idea that the Spirit on Jesus after his Jordan anointing and the Spirit on his disciples after their Pentecost infilling were essentially the same (just experienced in different epochs) that received Turner's special attention. And so the overall thesis that Turner's dissertation set out to present and defend was that according to Luke: "It would be misleading to speak of Jesus' experience of the Spirit as archetypal . . . The nexus of activities commenced by the Spirit through

---

239 n. 51). Nevertheless, some continue to present this distinction (e.g., Twelftree, *People of the Spirit*, 94).

20. Stronstad, *Charismatic Theology*, 68.

21. So Witherington, *Acts*, 569–70. Bruce, *Acts*, 363, disagrees: "Had Luke meant to indicate that they were disciples of John . . . he would have said so explicitly."

Jesus following his baptism and until his death, has points of contact with the nexus of activities commenced by the Spirit in and through the disciples of Jesus after Pentecost—their circles overlap—but the differences are more marked than the similarities; the intersect of the circles is minimal."[22] Perhaps more directly relevant to Pentecostal understandings of Acts, Turner concluded that the reception of the Spirit was not soteriologically necessary, while at the same time denying that the Spirit as given at Pentecost was merely an optional extra. His position at this time was closer to classical Pentecostalism than to Dunn. This proximity is all the more clear when Turner's 1980 work is compared to his 1996 work (see later). In 1980, he regarded the gift of the Spirit as merely "potentially important to the Christian life of the individual."[23]

Turner on Dunn's Approach

I will now consider Turner's specific criticisms of Dunn's approach and findings. In his introduction to Dunn's contribution to studies in Lukan pneumatology, Turner criticizes Dunn's method before considering any of his particular exegetical observations. According to Turner, in Dunn's exegesis of Luke, "the categories he has used in describing the Spirit are substantially pauline ones." Here we find common ground with Stronstad, of whose work Turner is, at this stage, unaware.[24] Turner continues: "Indeed, it is hard to believe that Dunn has avoided the temptation of reading Luke's endeavour through pauline spectacles. This does not prevent him, by any means, from criticising Luke—but the standard by which he judges Luke is itself a pauline reading of the NT."[25] An example of Turner's concern emerges early: Dunn's understanding of Jesus' Spirit reception beside the Jordan, by which reception Jesus is aided to resist evil and subjectively experiences sonship to God, "would undoubtedly overplay the parallels between (e.g.) Rom 8.14 and the 'ordeal' narrative."[26] In response Turner makes a point that is vital to several Pentecostal formulations of New Testament pneumatology,

22. Turner, "Luke and the Spirit," 185.

23. Ibid., 178; cf. 179, 186.

24. Despite the detail of argument and the thoroughness of research evidenced in his 1980 dissertation, Turner's bibliography does not include Stronstad's 1975 thesis.

25. Ibid., 28.

26. Ibid., 83. Turner continues to express this concern in 1996 (e.g., Turner, *Power from on High*, 329).

but that Turner will himself go on in subsequent years to suppress. It is that Dunn has regarded "receiving the Spirit" as in effect a fixed, technical term in the New Testament. It "does not seem to occur to Dunn . . . that Luke is using the language of 'receiving (the gift of) the Spirit' at a quite different level from that of Paul, and that he might be doing so intentionally."[27] In other words, when Luke and Paul wrote their works, language concerning receiving the Spirit was still fluid. This subject will be explored in more detail later (see chapter 4).

Turner on Dunn's Exegesis

Turning now to Turner's critique of Dunn's exegesis, Turner's first significant criticism of Dunn concerns the impact of Jesus' own Spirit reception on his disciples. For Dunn, the epoch of Jesus was one in which only Jesus himself enjoyed new covenant life, by virtue of his Spirit reception. The disciples, in contrast, still experienced old covenant life until Pentecost.[28] But, Turner objects, this "flatly contradicts the view of the Spirit on Jesus that we have attributed to Luke."[29] In two ways, for Turner, the disciples also personally benefited from the Spirit on Jesus during his earthly ministry. First, there was an overflow, so to speak, of the Spirit through Jesus onto them, such that they also benefited from the advantages of new covenant life at this time. Turner cites, as one of many examples, Luke 10:20, about the disciples' names being written in heaven. Dunn's assertion that this must refer to old covenant blessings "will not do: Jesus' statement is anchored to its eschatological context and assures participation in the salvation which is breaking in through the disciples' activity."[30] With regard to this gracious "overflow," Turner concludes: "Luke considered the 'life' of the kingdom, a deep inner sense of divine forgiveness and of sonship, to be realities experienced within the period of Jesus' ministry by those who belonged to the circle of his disciples and, to some extent, by those beyond it who nevertheless believed Jesus' preaching."[31]

27. Turner, "Luke and the Spirit," 27–28, quotation from 28.
28. Dunn, *Baptism*, 41–43.
29. Turner, "Luke and the Spirit," 97.
30. Ibid., 245 n. 43.
31. Ibid., 109.

Secondly, the disciples received power to engage in Jesus' mission (Luke 9:1; cf. 10:1–21) and this must be related to the Spirit. Despite the mention of power and authority at Luke 9:1, Turner is actually more interested in the pneumatological implications of Luke 10:1–21. First, he sees the sending out of the seventy or seventy-two as a reflection of Numbers 11:16–30, where the Spirit was transferred from Moses to seventy elders. Therefore, it is an implicit extension of the Spirit on Jesus to his disciples for their involvement in his mission.[32] Secondly, Jesus' joy "in the Holy Spirit" (Luke 10:21) was for Turner not just the work of the Spirit in Jesus' inner religious experience, but also Jesus' response to the work of the Spirit in and through the disciples who had just returned with good news of a successful mission (Luke 10:17).[33] Thus "Luke does not choose to say that the disciples 'received the Spirit' during Jesus' earthly sojourn, possibly to avoid confusion with what he says later concerning the pentecostal gift. But there is a very real sense in which such language could be applied to what he describes happening before the ascension . . . and this must affect our understanding of what Luke says about the descent of the Spirit at Pentecost."[34] In conclusion, Turner disagrees with Dunn's reading of the period of Jesus' ministry in Luke in two respects: the disciples experienced salvation through Jesus' own anointing of the Spirit; and they experienced the Spirit's work through them all, even if Luke did not use "Spirit reception language" of their acquisition of this gift.

Turner's other extended criticisms of Dunn relate to episodes recorded in Acts. In his account of Pentecost, Turner offers no sustained interaction with Dunn. His only argument concerns the "christological uniqueness" of Acts 2:33. As he puts it, "The Spirit is elsewhere exclusively the gift of God, the extension of *his* personality and vitality—to say that Jesus *execheen touto* ['poured out this'] (2.33) makes Jesus Lord, not merely of men, but also of God's Spirit."[35] Turner seeks to highlight this uniqueness by indicating that no pre-Christian Judaism—not even the Judaism expressed in John the Baptist's promise—should be understood to suggest that a coming messiah would actually grant the Spirit.

---

32. Ibid., 113.

33. Ibid., 86–88. So too, more emphatically, Turner, "Prayer in the Gospels and Acts," 63.

34. Turner, "Luke and the Spirit," 112.

35. Ibid., 126; italics original.

With reference to the Baptist's predictions, Turner disagrees with Dunn's claim that certain Jews had already begun to express their hopes for the coming messiah to do roughly this, and that it was only a small conceptual step for John to offer his fully developed prediction.[36] So Turner concludes that the Baptist's promise speaks rather "of the overwhelming deluge of Spirit-and-fire that will attend the coming of the Anointed in judgment."[37] We will return later in this chapter to Turner's understanding of John's promise, for it relates to his reading of Acts 11:16 and its context.

Dunn again comes within Turner's line of fire in his account of the Samaritan episode of Acts 8. Here, according to Turner, Dunn offers an "extreme of interpretation."[38] In a lengthy rebuttal of Dunn's exegesis, Turner includes the following points.

a.   Luke clearly viewed Philip's ministry as proficient. (For example in Acts 8:5, where "the expression concerned ['proclaimed the Christ'] . . . is to convey to the reader that Philip delivered the normal christian message."[39])

b.   There is nothing pejorative in Luke's use of *homothumadon* ("with one accord"): quite the opposite. The context indicates that Luke was seeking to "emphasize Philip's success in Samaria . . . not the samaritan [*sic*] failure."[40]

c.   In contrast to Acts 18:26, where Priscilla and Aquila "improved" Apollos' theology, the Jerusalem apostles on arrival in Samaria neither corrected nor developed what Philip had preached. In fact, their message to the converts, other than to Simon, was not recorded at all. We are simply told that the

---

36. While Dunn's reading of various Qumran documents suggests to him that this community had already come close to expecting a messiah who would grant God's Spirit, Turner plausibly dismantles Dunn's reading. Also, Turner regards *T. Jud.* 24:3, which does speak of a coming messiah granting S/spirit, as a later Christian interpolation in an original Jewish text.

37. Ibid., 127. Turner's discussion here relates not to Dunn's *Baptism*, but to Dunn's 1972 article, "Spirit and Fire Baptism." Turner argues with Dunn concerning his understanding of the Baptist's promise at greater length in Turner, *Power from on High*, 179–80.

38. Turner, "Luke and the Spirit," 162.

39. Ibid., 163.

40. Ibid.

apostles heard that Samaria had accepted God's word (Acts 8:14).

d. Dunn's hypothesis that Samaritan belief was mere "intellectual assent" "is at best oversubtle. Luke makes no distinction between believing an evangelist and believing God: to give heed to the former is to hear the God who speaks through him."[41]

e. Simon cannot be regarded as unconverted. Turner offers Ananias and Sapphira, with an exclamation mark, as examples of Jesus' followers who nevertheless allowed themselves to be drawn into gross sin. Simon was not told by Peter that he had no part in the "word" of Christianity (Acts 8:21), but that he had no part in "this affair" of bestowing the Spirit.[42]

All this leads Turner to conclude: "the very fact of the separation of baptism from receiving the Spirit here, and the characteristics of Luke's description, favour the view that he did not identify receiving the Spirit as the gift of messianic salvation itself, but as one particular nexus within it."[43] However, despite this firm disagreement with Dunn, Turner makes an observation that in later years will take his thinking away from classical Pentecostalism and closer to Dunn's position. It is that Luke deliberately included an "awkward explanation" at Acts 8:16 to indicate that he "cannot have believed the Samaritan episode was typical at all."[44] Turner neither tells us what he regards as awkward about the explanation,[45] nor does he say what features in the narrative would have been regarded by Luke as unusual, but in later years Turner builds on this point significantly and is forthright that Acts 2:38 sets out the typical, normative experience of the Spirit in Christian initiation: it was the *delay* in Samaria that was abnormal.

In the case of Paul's conversion in Acts 9, Turner agrees with Dunn's conclusions. However, the Cornelius episode calls forth a different reaction to Dunn. Turner does not part company here as forcibly as he did

41. Ibid., 165. Precisely the same words reappear in Turner, *Power from on High*, 365.

42. Turner, "Luke and the Spirit," 166.

43. Ibid., 170; italics removed.

44. Ibid., 162.

45. In 1996, he does: if delay was normal, the explanation would be "redundant" (Turner, *Power from on High*, 360).

with respect to Acts 8, but nonetheless declares that "the argument is not tight enough to clinch Dunn's case."[46] After all, when Cornelius received the Spirit, the enablement was that of "charismatic speech," which is distinguishable from forgiveness. Also, neither in Acts 11:17–18 nor in Acts 15:8–9 was receiving the Spirit equated with receiving new covenant life. Rather, the Spirit's arrival was an attestation of this new life.[47]

In his discussion of the Ephesian Spirit reception (Acts 19:1–6), Turner refers explicitly to Dunn only minimally (in three footnotes), using him in affirmation of his own exegesis. However, there is implicit interaction with Dunn regarding the wording of Paul's first question to the Ephesian disciples. The question, "decidedly more lucan in form than pauline," probably indicates the looser connection in Luke's mind between coming to faith and receiving the Spirit than in the mind of the epistolary Paul.

In all, Turner in 1980 mounts a fairly robust criticism of Dunn, and one that, at this point, is generally consonant with a classical Pentecostal doctrine of subsequence. As we shall soon see, however, Turner later revises his views in significant ways.

HOWARD ERVIN

It emerged in chapter 1 that, of all the works reviewed in this book, Ervin's is the most direct reply to Dunn's *Baptism*. In his critique of Dunn's thesis, Ervin offers criticisms of many of Dunn's specific exegetical points, but also, scattered amongst these, criticisms of Dunn's overall methods.

Ervin on Dunn's Methods

Ervin's first criticism is in his introduction: "Implicit in his methodology are metaphysical assumptions about the nature of spiritual reality."[48] These assumptions form the basis of Dunn's anti-Pentecostalism. Dunn has not begun with a fair and unbiased[49] perusal of the New Testament, but has allowed his exegesis of the relevant passages to be flawed by a view of Spirit and matter as "logically quantified into discontinu-

46. Turner, "Luke and the Spirit," 172.

47. Ibid., 172–73.

48. Ervin, *Conversion-Initiation*, viii.

49. Note Ervin's accusation of "strongly worded anti-Pentecostal . . . bias," in ibid., 15.

ous, even antithetical, spheres of God's presence and activity."[50] This dichotomy in Dunn's mind has led to his rejection of Pentecostalism, for "the phenomenology of the Pentecostal experience precludes quantifying reality into discontinuous spheres of Spirit and matter."[51] This first criticism apparently misrepresents Dunn's position. Dunn may be "anti-Pentecostal" but, as I stated in the previous chapter, he is certainly not "anti-charismatic." Dunn's view of Spirit reception as portrayed in the New Testament is that it was an equipping "with power," "for service and witness," a "dramatic," "manifest," "vivid" experience visited with "external accompaniments."[52] Ervin, along with some other Pentecostals described in this work, seems to have failed to appreciate the degree of sympathy that Dunn offers the Pentecostal position on this point. Dunn declares openly in his introduction to *Baptism* that "the Pentecostal's belief in the dynamic and experiential nature of Spirit-baptism is well founded,"[53] and in his conclusion that "Pentecostal teaching on spiritual gifts, including glossolalia, while still unbalanced, is much more soundly based on the NT than is generally recognised."[54] It is not implausible to suggest, indeed, that Dunn's thesis challenges some non-Pentecostals as much as Pentecostals, for it declares to someone who has not experienced a vivid empowering: "The New Testament questions whether you are a Christian."[55]

Ervin's second criticism is best set out in his own words: "The real question at issue here is a methodological one. Both the conversion-initiation and the Pentecostal advocates appeal to Scripture and to logic . . . A fundamental difference, however, is the added appeal of the Pentecostal witness to a personal experience with the charisms of the Spirit subsequent to conversion. This appeal to a 'Pentecostal' experience does not pre-empt the first two criteria but is understood as a corrobora-

---

50. Ibid., 82.

51. Ibid., 83.

52. Dunn, *Baptism*, 24, 54, 100, 105, 132; cf. Dunn, "Rediscovering the Spirit (2)," 64–65. See also Macchia, "Salvation and Spirit Baptism," 2–3.

53. Dunn, *Baptism*, 4.

54. Ibid., 229.

55. Stronstad also misrepresents Dunn on this point, for he writes of Dunn "attributing a soteriological rather than a charismatic significance to the gift of the Spirit" (Stronstad, *Charismatic Theology*, 62). Dunn actually attributes both to the Spirit, but prioritizes the soteriological aspect over the charismatic.

tive witness to the biblical integrity of the Pentecostal thesis."[56] Appeal to personal experience as a key to exegesis of a text cannot be dismissed without discussion. Indeed, experience in its broadest sense is the *only* source of the pre-understanding that a reader brings to a text and that enables the reader to understand the text.[57] However, personal experience must only be allowed to inform exegesis and not to determine it. For instance, the thought that, "I have never experienced a miracle; therefore miracles do not actually occur; therefore accounts of miracles cannot accurately reflect historical events" is inadmissible.[58] Rather, readers lacking personal experience of the subject matter in a text must content themselves with the realization that their understanding will be relatively uninformed. Ervin, with his repeated appeals to Pentecostal experience,[59] at least gives the impression that his experience might occasionally be determining his exegesis. This is a habit that is criticized from within the Pentecostal movement.[60] Even if this is not true of Ervin,[61] he is ill-advised in implying that Dunn is unqualified either to exegete passages relating to Spirit reception or to criticize Pentecostal interpretations of those passages, on account of Dunn's supposed lack of a subsequent charismatic experience of the Spirit.

Ervin's third criticism is that Dunn breaks the very rule that he himself lays down for biblical theologians (and accuses Pentecostals of disobeying[62]), that they must seek to understand each biblical author individually before attempting a synthesis of biblical thought.[63] At times, Ervin reflects Stronstad's and Turner's criticism that Dunn reads Luke while wearing Pauline glasses.[64] However, Ervin's chief complaint is that Dunn blurs the distinctives between Luke's and John's pneumatolo-

---

56. Ervin, *Conversion-Initiation*, 23.

57. See Thiselton, *Two Horizons*, 103–6, e.g., "understanding is profoundly conditioned by our own experience" (ibid., 106).

58. Cf. Thiselton, *Two Horizons*, 72–73.

59. Ervin, *Conversion-Initiation*, 6, 23, 26, 27, 64, 72.

60. E.g., Fee, *Gospel and Spirit*, 86–87; Menzies, "Methodology of Pentecostal Theology," 12.

61. To be fair, Ervin writes clearly in *Spirit-Baptism* of the difference between experience-*dictated* exegesis and experience-*informed* exegesis (ibid., ix).

62. Dunn, *Baptism*, 39.

63. Ervin, *Conversion-Initiation*, 25–26.

64. E.g., ibid., 27.

gies.[65] At this point, it must be noted that Ervin also breaks this rule. A clear example is in his discussion of the Ephesian twelve (Acts 19:1–7). John 16:8 is used to show the Spirit's presence in their conviction, and 1 Corinthians 12:3 serves to display the Spirit's presence in their baptism in water (for they must have confessed Christ's lordship in this event). Thereby, Acts 19:6 is shown to portray something other than their initial "salvific" experience of the Spirit.[66]

In conclusion to this section about Dunn's methods, Ervin's criticisms do not carry weight. While the first is apparently based on a misunderstanding, the latter two serve even to cast suspicion on Ervin's own methods.

Ervin on Dunn's Exegesis

Studying the Jordan and Pentecost outpourings, Ervin engages surprisingly little with Dunn's exegesis. He rather dismisses Dunn's understanding and then presents his own. Ervin repeats that Dunn's view of Christ's anointing as primarily initiatory lacks the support of "hard exegetical evidence,"[67] but does not attempt to show how the evidence that Dunn presents is suspect. Similarly, in considering Pentecost, it is really only in an excursus on *hē epangelia* ("the promise") referred to in Luke 24:49; Acts 1:4; 2:33, 38–39 that he directly tackles Dunn's exegesis. He rightly criticizes Dunn, who points out that Luke and Paul often used *epangelia* to refer to God's covenant promise, for failing to show that Luke used it with that referent in these verses. Ervin is correct in pointing out, rather, that Luke 24:49 identified this promise with "power from on high," an identification confirmed by Acts 1:4–8; 2:16–19.[68] However, in his discussion of the conversion of the Samaritans, Paul, and the Ephesians, we find Dunn's exegesis more thoroughly examined.

Dunn, writes Ervin, is wrong to see the Samaritans' initial faith as defective.

    a. *pisteuein* ("to believe") with a proposition or person as dative object does not necessarily indicate mere intellectual assent. "Acts 24:14 cannot be pressed on grammatical grounds to

---

65. E.g., ibid., 70–71.
66. Ibid., 64.
67. Ibid., 5, 10.
68. Ibid., 19–20.

support any claim that Paul simply gave intellectual assent to the Law and the Prophets."[69] That the Samaritans' response was more than intellectual is shown by their public commitment to Jesus through baptism in water: a baptism accepted as valid by the apostles.

b.   They did not just believe Philip, but Philip *as he preached the gospel* (*episteusan tō Philippō euangelizomenō*—Acts 8:12).

c.   The Samaritans were not exceptionally superstitious, as is evidenced by contemporary Jewish magical texts and by the text of Acts itself (e.g., Acts 19:13–16).

d.   Simon was not unconverted (and therefore neither were the other new believers). Dunn's analogy between Acts 8:23 and Deuteronomy 29:18 makes this clear, for Deuteronomy 29:18 spoke of those whose heart turned away from the Lord.

Ervin's overall exegesis of this passage is much more convincing than Dunn's, and introduces some details of exegesis beyond those already offered by Turner.

In his examination of Paul's conversion, Ervin disagrees with Dunn's translation of *kurie* as "Sir." Elsewhere in Acts where *kurie* was used, the context demands the translation "Lord." Even at Acts 10:4, "Sir" is a dubious suggestion: "In the numinous-charged atmosphere of an angelic visitation, surely the vocative *kurie* on the lips of Cornelius is pregnant with the sense of the Holy."[70] Thus also at Acts 9:5, as at Acts 7:56–59; 9:10; 10:14; 22:19, *kurie* "must be understood in the theological context of the accompanying theophany."[71] Furthermore, Paul's question at Acts 9:5 was rhetorical, not ignorant. Paul's conversion *began* at the stoning of Stephen (Acts 22:20): he probably heard Stephen's final words. The "Damascus-road experience marked Paul's final capitulation to Jesus as Lord."[72] As to Ananias' use of *adelphe* ("brother"), Acts 9:13–15 shows that any sense of brotherhood Ananias felt with Paul arose not from Paul's Judaism but from his relationship to Christ. Ervin's interesting points do cast some doubt on Dunn's arguments. However, Ervin might

69. Ibid., 29.

70. Ibid., 43.

71. Ibid., 43.

72. Ibid., 44.

have been more thorough, for the force of Acts 22:16 and the symbolism of Paul's three day blindness *for Luke*[73] require explanation, if Ervin's claim that Luke portrayed Paul as converted on the Damascus road is to be accepted.

When considering the Ephesian disciples of Acts 19, Ervin does not follow Stronstad in claiming that the twelve were Christians before meeting Paul. For Ervin that matter is simple: "They were disciples of John."[74] Pursuing a different line of argument, that sees their status before Paul met them as irrelevant, Ervin stresses the subsequence of their Spirit reception, at Paul's laying on of hands, to their baptism in water, which baptism presupposed faith. Luke's genitive absolute (a Greek grammatical construction) in Acts 19:6 indicates the sequential, rather than the parenthetic, nature of Paul's laying on of hands, contrary to Dunn's claim.[75] "Conversion-initiation culminates in water baptism. The laying on of hands subsequent to water baptism is for the reception of the Holy Spirit for power-in-mission."[76] Is Ervin right? Certainly, the laying on of hands for reception of the Spirit was chronologically separate from water baptism in Samaria, and we do not know that laying on of hands was considered a part of New Testament baptismal procedure.[77] However, in the specific case of the Ephesians, to argue that Luke presented the placing of Paul's hands on them as something *other* than a part of their whole initiation procedure is implausible: whether or not the Ephesians were still in the water when Paul placed his hands on them, the time gap between their baptisms and his laying on of hands does not seem to have been significant.

In conclusion, Ervin believes that Luke kept separate what Dunn has joined together: salvation and the gift of the Spirit. Ervin's challenge to Dunn is argued along philosophical and experiential lines as well as exegetical ones. While the former arguments are not convincing, some of the latter ones carry weight. Ervin has further undermined Dunn's

---

73. Ervin tackles Dunn over the issue of Paul's blindness, but considers the most likely explanation (physiological rather than psychological) of the event, without considering Luke's view of that event (ibid., 45–46).

74. Ibid., 58.

75. Dunn, *Baptism*, 87.

76. Ervin, *Conversion-Initiation*, 66.

77. Beasley-Murray, *Baptism in the New Testament*, 123.

exegesis of Acts 8:4–25, and has placed important question marks against some of his other arguments.

DAVID PETTS

The response of David Petts is distinctive amongst those under review, not only in the impression it gives his readers of Petts' willingness to listen carefully to what Dunn is saying and weigh up sympathetically both sides of the argument, but also in the degree of agreement with Dunn that this process leads to. This agreement is obvious in his conclusion: "His [Dunn's] chief strength is that he has rightly drawn attention to the centrality of the gift of the Spirit in conversion-initiation. I believe Ervin is wrong to limit Christian initiation to repentance/faith and water baptism. We must with Dunn (and Acts 2:38) add the gift of the Spirit. But that is not to make the gift of the Spirit salvation itself. It is distinct from salvation as it is distinct from water-baptism. Yet it is intimately connected to both, and, in a sense, without it salvation, in the full NT use of the term, is incomplete."[78] As these concluding words disclose, it is largely the force of Acts 2:38 that leads Petts, while not identifying Spirit reception with salvation, nevertheless to see Spirit reception as an integral part of Christian initiation. This verse is important, for Petts seems to accept Dunn's opinion that "Luke probably intends Acts 2:38 to establish the pattern and norm for Christian conversion-initiation."[79] Pointing out that the gift of the Spirit mentioned here was the charismatic endowment that the 120 had just received, Petts understands from this verse that "the suggestion that the gift is merely *available* after baptism is inadequate." He concludes that "conversion (in the full sense of the NT understanding of that term) is not complete without it."[80]

Despite this agreement with Dunn, Petts does disagree on substantial points. First, for Petts, Dunn has seriously underestimated the connection in Luke's mind between receiving the Spirit and missionary enabling. Petts suggests that such a devaluing has occurred because Dunn has failed to devote a section of his work to the exegesis of Acts' opening verses. Petts can find no fault with a Pentecostal understanding that the "power" of Acts 1:8 is both the Spirit baptism of Acts 1:5 and the

78. Petts, "Baptism in the Holy Spirit," 87.
79. Dunn, *Baptism*, 90.
80. Petts, "Baptism in the Holy Spirit," 60; italics original.

promised "gift" of Acts 1:4, for Luke 24:49 identified the promise with the power. Petts disagrees with Dunn's claim that Luke never directly associated Spirit reception with promised power.[81] Petts' observation is astute and accurate. There is serious inattention in Dunn's work to Acts 1:4–8. If, as Dunn rightly observes, Acts 2:38 has programmatic import for Christian initiation, then surely Acts 1:8 is equally programmatic in Luke's eyes for the significance of Spirit reception within that initiation.[82]

Secondly, Petts criticizes Dunn for identifying reception of forgiveness with reception of the Spirit in Luke's pneumatology. This is clearest in his study of the Cornelius episode. For Petts, Luke's apposition of Acts 10:44 with Acts 10:43 does not imply that "Cornelius at that moment reached out in faith to God for *forgiveness* and received, as God's response, the *Holy Spirit*."[83] Rather, "Cornelius reached out for forgiveness and received *forgiveness and* the Holy Spirit, for the evidence of the Spirit's coming is described by Luke as glossolalia (10:46) which is nowhere in the NT seen as evidence of forgiveness."[84]

Thirdly, Petts does not view Spirit reception, as presented by Luke, as necessarily contemporaneous with initial faith. Not surprisingly, he follows Stronstad, Turner, and Ervin in a firm rejection of Dunn's exegesis of Acts 8:4–25.[85] Like Ervin, he concentrates on the meaning of *pisteuein* ("to believe") with the dative, and accepts Ervin's arguments. Unlike Stronstad, who views the temporal separation between belief and Spirit reception as "typical,"[86] Petts echoes Turner's opinion when he states that, "Luke intends us to understand the Samaritan situation as abnormal."[87]

In his investigation of the Ephesian episode, Petts' contribution is significant, for he goes beyond Ervin in considering the implications of Paul's opening question. For Petts, the Pentecostal position does not stand or fall by the nature of the aorist participle *pisteusantes* ("believ-

---

81. Ibid., 50–51.

82. The same rejoinder will need to be offered below to Max Turner, *Power from on High*.

83. Dunn, *Baptism*, 80; italics original.

84. Petts, "Baptism in the Holy Spirit," 70; italics original.

85. Ibid., 61–66.

86. Stronstad, *Charismatic Theology*, 65.

87. Petts, "Baptism in the Holy Spirit," 65.

ing") in Acts 19:2—antecedent ("after you believed") or coincident ("when you believed"). Even if it is coincident, and the question suggests that it is normal to receive the Spirit when one first believes, the very fact that the question was asked suggests "that it is at least *possible* to believe without receiving the Spirit."[88] Here Petts is again on the same ground as Turner. The latter points out that the appeal of the question might have been *ad hominem*, but considers nonetheless that the question probably does reflect Lukan pneumatology.[89] At this point, Petts is much more convincing than Dunn, who appeals to Paul's second question as evidence that "the Spirit is received in connection with baptism"[90] and that therefore according to Luke "it is Paul's doctrine that a man receives the Spirit *when* he believes."[91] In fact, Paul's doubts about the nature of their baptism arose not because they had not received the Spirit (presumably this fact was evident to him—hence his first question, which expected a "No"), but because they were unaware that the Spirit was now available.[92] In conclusion, Petts' overall response is impressive, both because of his fairness and willingness to listen to Dunn and because of his ability to pinpoint serious weaknesses in Dunn's exegesis and presentation.

JAMES SHELTON

Shelton's response to Dunn is only detailed and sustained in an appendix entitled "Jesus, John, the Spirit, and the New Age." In an argument that concentrates on Luke's use of his sources, Shelton challenges Dunn's belief that the arrival of the Spirit in Jesus' life at the Jordan River marked the arrival of a whole new epoch in salvation history.

Shelton accepts that three eras of salvation history were obvious in the source material Luke redacted, but argues that Luke himself minimized the distinctions between them. Luke depicted the epochs "not as separate voices but as one voice steadily increasing in volume."[93] As Shelton writes elsewhere, the only pneumatological difference for Luke

---

88. Ibid., 74.

89. Turner, "Luke and the Spirit," 175, and see above.

90. Dunn, *Baptism*, 86.

91. Ibid., 87; italics original.

92. Turner, "Luke and the Spirit," 174; Bruce, *Acts*, 406.

93. Shelton, *Mighty in Word and Deed*, 173.

between the epochs was quantitative rather than qualitative.[94] In seeing a rigid distinction of epochs in Luke's account, Dunn has repeated
Conzelmann's mistake.[95] Shelton's main argument is that Luke did not
present John the Baptist as an "old epoch" character. Luke 16:16, for instance, does not squeeze John exclusively into the old epoch, for *mechri*
("until") and *apo tote* ("since then") allow overlap.[96] Rather, John, like
the other Spirit-filled individuals in the infancy narratives, received the
Spirit to do precisely what Jesus and his followers received the Spirit
to do: to offer inspired speech.[97] Shelton also debates with Dunn about
Christ's conception, which Shelton cannot see as an event within the old
age or old covenant. He believes that "to separate the advent of the incar-
nation itself from the new age appears totally arbitrary." So the anointing
at the Jordan River could not be the start of the new age, but a "sub-unit"
or "subsection" of the new era.[98]

Shelton's argument here lies between those of Dunn and Menzies
(see below). He is helpful in acknowledging that the Spirit's activity recorded in Luke 1–2 was not the explosive arrival of the new age suggested
by Menzies. It was rather the first audible sound of a massive crescendo.
However, he underestimates the sharp increase in volume that occurred
beside the Jordan River. Luke did not present Jesus' anointing as a mere
"sub-unit" of the new age. This was the unique anointing of the unique
Son for a unique purpose: not just to announce forgiveness and release—
many prophets before Jesus had done that—but now actually to deliver
forgiveness and release (Luke 4:18).[99]

Shelton's other areas of interaction with Dunn are less sustained.
He offers a noteworthy response in his analyses of Pentecost, of Paul's
conversion, of Cornelius' reception of the Spirit, and of the Ephesian
reception. In his study of the events at Pentecost, Shelton takes up the
charge that Dunn has read Luke as if his words were by Paul. Shelton is
more specific about this: the mistake has been to assume that both Luke

94. Ibid., 16, 26: "Peter . . . described Pentecost as unique not in character but in
scope" (ibid., 26).

95. Ibid., 173.

96. Ibid., 167–68.

97. Ibid., 171.

98. Ibid., 172–73; quotation from 172.

99. Shelton does attribute one unique aspect to Jesus' anointing in Luke: it was
kingly (ibid., 55 n. 5).

and Paul were seeking to answer the same question, whereas in fact while Paul was showing how one is a Christian, Luke was expounding how one witnesses. For Luke, the disciples "apparently" came to belief through the events recorded in Luke 24: "It seems incredible that Luke would present the disciples as witnesses of Jesus' death, resurrection, and ascension; as recipients of his commission . . . and blessing . . . ; as joyful . . . , united . . . ; and devoted to prayer . . . ; and yet not see them as converted."[100]

In describing Paul's conversion, Shelton tentatively suggests his future theme: Luke was perhaps deliberately ambiguous. Nevertheless, Luke probably understood Paul as converted on the Damascus road: it was not Ananias but Jesus himself, on the road, who revealed Jesus as Lord to Paul; Paul was in prayer before Ananias' arrival; Ananias called Paul "brother" before he received the Spirit.[101] In the cases of the Gentile and Ephesian outpourings of Acts 10 and 19, Shelton grapples briefly with Dunn's exegesis of Acts 11:18 and 19:1. Dunn has read in too much. Acts 11:18 is not a clear indication that "repentance unto life" occurred only when Cornelius heard Peter. Acts 19:1 does not distinguish the Ephesian disciples from Christians.[102] In both descriptions, rather, Luke was ambiguous, failing to delineate clearly the relationship between conversion and Spirit reception, precisely because this was not his primary interest. The ambiguity is most obvious in Acts 10–11. Cornelius was a man whose activities already "met with divine approval"; yet Peter's message would lead to his salvation.[103]

While weak at points (Paul's praying was no indication of prior commitment to Jesus: all Jews prayed!), Shelton's work is fairest concerning the *lack* of clarity in some of Luke's descriptions. He also offers a reasonable explanation for this ambiguity: "Why is Luke not clearer? It is primarily because the role of the Spirit in conversion is not his major interest."[104] While admitting that disappointment may result, Shelton offers this warning: "Luke's redactional interests must be respected, and we must not read too much into the text concerning the converted state

100. Ibid., 128.

101. Ibid., 131, following Ervin.

102. Ibid., 151 n. 24, following Stronstad.

103. Ibid., 131–32; see Acts 10:4; 11:14.

104. Ibid., 135.

of the recipients of the Holy Spirit since Luke himself does not clarify the point."[105]

In summary, Shelton offers little direct response to Dunn that goes beyond those already reviewed. His counter-argument concerning the idea of three separate epochs in Luke's salvation history is helpful, offering more nuanced exegesis of Luke's presentation. Beyond that, he points out successfully that Luke is simply not as clear as Dunn on the one hand and Pentecostals on the other might like. Luke is not setting out to answer their questions (!) but is pursuing a purpose that does not involve delineating precisely the relationship between Spirit reception and conversion. Luke's readers are left to fill in gaps, draw inferences, and even at times make guesses.

ROBERT MENZIES

Menzies' is the most thorough response thus far of those under review: being more recent than those so far discussed, it is able to incorporate the insights of the older works into its own;[106] it is also one of the longest, being only the second to represent doctoral work (the first being that of Turner). Menzies' main thesis, developing and adapting the work of Eduard Schweizer and of Turner's doctorate, is that New Testament pneumatologies developed along disparate lines, meaning that Luke's view of the Spirit was neither identical to the pneumatology visible in his sources, such as Mark's Gospel and Q, nor identical to what emerges from Paul's letters or later writings. In particular, Luke's view of the Spirit was remarkably narrow, distinctive for what it excluded: for Luke, the Spirit did not grant recipients new life; did not enable them to perform miracles; did not have significant ethical impact; and did not primarily benefit these recipients at all—the Spirit was given *for others*. What the Spirit *was* given for was entirely prophetic: primarily the missionary witness of the growing church. Unsurprisingly, given such a narrow view of the Spirit's functions in Lukan pneumatology, Menzies' position lies at the opposite extreme to that of Dunn, even further away from Dunn in the spectrum than Stronstad is. While there are elements of Menzies' thesis with which it is possible to disagree, he has made a great contribu-

---

105. Ibid., 136.

106. Menzies' bibliography to *Development* includes works by Stronstad, Turner, and Ervin but not Petts. Menzies, *Empowered for Witness*, contains one brief reference to Shelton (ibid., 35 n. 6).

tion to the whole discussion and no student of Lukan pneumatology can afford to ignore what he has written.

Menzies' doctoral dissertation was first published in 1991 as *The Development of Early Christian Pneumatology*. When it was republished in 1994 as *Empowered for Witness*, this was in a somewhat revised form. Where appropriate, I will give page references to both works in my citations. My review will follow the structure of Menzies' analysis of Dunn's main arguments.[107] For Menzies, Dunn supports his position with three primary claims: Jesus' anointing at the Jordan marked primarily his initiation into the new messianic age; the Pentecostal gift constituted the new covenant; and all further receptions of the Spirit were initiating experiences into the new age and covenant.

Jordan: Dawn of the Messianic Age?

Menzies disagrees sharply with Dunn's statement that Jesus' anointing at the Jordan River "initiates the messianic age and initiates Jesus into the messianic age."[108] For Menzies, a simple observation undermines Dunn's claim: "when the eschatological nature of Luke 1–2 is recognized and Conzelmann's rigid *heilsgeschichtlich* ['salvation-historical'] scheme is discarded, it cannot be maintained that Jesus' baptism is the *pivot* of salvation history—the point at which Jesus enters the new age."[109] Menzies views the outburst of prophetic activity recorded in Luke 1–2 as the dawn of the messianic age.[110] Jesus' (prophetic) anointing is in continuity with this, and while it obviously is a new beginning, it is only "the inauguration of Jesus' messianic task."[111] Menzies' reasons for these claims must be carefully assessed.

Menzies' assertion that Luke presents his nativity narratives as the dawning of the new age rests upon his understanding of Jewish pneumatology at the time Luke wrote. Conducting an extensive survey of early Jewish literature and traditions, Menzies presents the following picture.

107. Menzies, *Development*, 31–34; *Empowered for Witness*, 30–33.

108. Dunn, *Baptism*, 25. Dunn's observation concerns the synoptic view of Christ, of which Luke's description forms a wholehearted contribution (ibid., 26–32). Menzies' explicit disagreement concerns Luke's portrayal.

109. Menzies, *Development*, 153; *Empowered for Witness*, 138; italics original.

110. Menzies, *Development*, 131; *Empowered for Witness*, 120. Similarly, see Hill, *Greek Words*, 254.

111. Menzies, *Development*, 153; *Empowered for Witness*, 138.

God's Spirit was understood as the source of prophetic inspiration, and thus was often and suitably termed *the Spirit of prophecy*. The Spirit was not normally seen as the power to perform miracles or to live uprightly before God. Outstanding leaders had been endowed with the Spirit of prophecy in the past, but this period was the age of prophetic silence.[112] The Jews looked forward to a new messianic age, when both the Messiah and his people would be anointed with the Spirit of prophecy. As generally understood, this endowment would not be soteriologically necessary.[113] Viewed against this background, the superficial plausibility of Menzies' argument about Luke 1–2 is obvious: any marked renewal of prophetic activity would be evidence of the new messianic age, and this is precisely what Luke presented in his first two chapters. More careful consideration, however, questions Menzies' reasoning.

First, is contemporary *Jewish* pneumatology as relevant for Lukan studies as Menzies implies? It is by no means certain that Luke was a Jew. While he has traditionally been viewed as a Gentile,[114] partly on account of Colossians 4:11–14, modern scholarship is divided.[115] Secondly, and importantly, Luke's intended readers were not exclusively, and probably not mainly, Jewish. While the identity of Theophilus remains a mystery,[116] the internal evidence of Luke-Acts shows a great interest in Gentiles.[117] Contemporary scholarly opinions concerning the identity of the intended readers of Luke-Acts vary between "Gentile Christians in a predominantly Gentile setting"[118] and, at the other extreme, God-fearers.[119] But none goes further than this and speaks of a predominantly Jewish audience.

---

112. How silent this "silence" was is disputed. For Dunn's view, see Dunn, "Baptism Yet Once More," 10; for a good discussion of the issues, see Wenk, *Community-Forming Power*, 112–33.

113. Menzies, *Development*, 51–112; *Empowered for Witness*, 49–102; cf. Stronstad, *Charismatic Theology*, 27–32. (Only in later Qumran and wisdom literature was possession of the Spirit seen as fundamental to one's walk with God.)

114. Nolland, *Luke 1—9:20*, xxxii.

115. Fitzmyer, *Gospel according to Luke (I–IX)*, 42.

116. Nolland, *Luke 1—9:20*, 10: *Theophilus* was a common name among both Jews and Greeks.

117. Summers, *Commentary on Luke*, 12; Bruce, *Acts*, 12.

118. Fitzmyer, *Gospel according to Luke (I–IX)*, 59.

119. Nolland, *Luke 1—9:20*, xxxii.

Secondly, and accepting for the sake of argument the full importance of contemporary Jewish expectations in the study of Luke's pneumatology, the precise nature of these expectations must be borne in
mind. There were two parallel hopes: of a unique Messiah endowed with
the Spirit,[120] and of a universal outpouring of the Holy Spirit on God's
people.[121] These may be said to be the hallmarks, pneumatologically, of
the coming messianic age, and it will be noticed that Luke 1–2 fulfills
neither of these criteria. The one revealed by the Spirit (Luke 2:27) and
by the angel (Luke 2:11) as the unique Messiah remained unendowed;
similarly the outpouring of the Spirit was not yet universal. Five characters were recorded as having the Spirit, either temporarily or permanently.[122] This is of course significant, but other characters regarded as major
(e.g., Joseph) and as godly (e.g., the shepherds [Luke 2:20] and Anna
[Luke 2:36–37]) were not. By Menzies' own criteria, Luke 1–2 must be
regarded as the pre-dawn pallor in the sky, or, to change the metaphor, as
birth-pangs of the messianic age.[123]

We must now turn to another of Menzies' observations that, for
him, undermines Dunn's view of the Jordan anointing. Dunn is wrong,
suggests Menzies, to follow Conzelmann in seeing a rigid three-epoch
scheme in Luke's history of salvation. In respect to pneumatology, Dunn
portrays the Spirit in the epoch of Israel as the Spirit of prophecy. In the
messianic era the Spirit takes on a new function, ushering in the new
covenant.[124] So the issue here is the *function* of the Spirit. Menzies, of
course, agrees with Dunn that Luke portrayed the Spirit in his first two
chapters as the Spirit of prophecy. But in contrast to Dunn he believes
that Luke portrayed the Spirit on Jesus as still the Spirit of prophecy.

120. Menzies, *Development*, 71–73; Menzies, *Empowered for Witness*, 66–67; Hill,
Greek Words, 232; Schweizer, *Holy Spirit*, 41; Heron, *Holy Spirit*, 23–25; Stronstad,
Charismatic Theology, 30–31. Passages adduced for this view include *1 En.* 49:3; 62:2;
Pss. Sol. 17:37; 18:7; *T. Levi* 18:7; *T. Jud.* 24:2. The possibility of Christian interpolation in
these texts is well recognized (e.g., Schweizer, *Holy Spirit*, 41; Heron, *Holy Spirit*, 24).

121. Menzies, *Development*, 104–5; Menzies, *Empowered for Witness*, 95–96; Hill,
Greek Words, 232–33. Both cite *Num. Rab.* 15:25.

122. John (Luke 1:15); Mary (Luke 1:35); Elizabeth (Luke 1:41); Zechariah (Luke
1:67); and Simeon (Luke 2:25).

123. Similarly, Stronstad, *Charismatic Theology*, 38–45: the prophetic renewal *her-
alds* the age's dawn. Stronstad has, however, more recently offered the useful observation that the arrival of the Spirit in the lives of male and female, old and young, was a
foretaste of the universal outpouring to come (Stronstad, *Baptized and Filled*, 21).

124. Dunn, *Baptism*, 31–32.

There was no new function of the Spirit on Jesus that warrants viewing Christ's ministry as belonging to a different epoch from, say, John the Baptist's. Rather, "Luke's pneumatology emphasizes the fundamental continuity which unites his story of fulfillment."[125]

Menzies takes his main evidence from Luke 4, where the Nazareth sermon pursues the theme of the Jordan anointing, as Luke highlighted with his "redactional bridge" about Christ's fullness of the Spirit (Luke 4:1, 14).[126] Menzies does not merely follow Stronstad and Ervin[127] in stating that Isaiah 61:1–2 is presented as an explanation of what happened at the Jordan River. It is Menzies' belief that Luke, as opposed to his sources, altered the Septuagint to highlight the prophetic nature of the endowment Christ had just received. In particular, the phrase *iasasthai tous suntetrimmenous tēn kardian* ("to heal the crushed in heart": Isaiah 61:1d, LXX) was omitted, because it would directly have associated the Spirit of prophecy with miraculous healing, and *aposteilai tethrausmenous en aphesei* ("to send [the] oppressed into release": Isaiah 58:6d, LXX) was "imported" from Isaiah 58:6 to Luke 4:18, to declare that Christ's anointed preaching would have power to liberate people from their sins.[128]

This last argument actually seems to play into Dunn's hands, for Luke 4:18–19 does not declare that the Christ is sent merely to proclaim release for the oppressed, but actually to do the releasing.[129] If the anointing Christ received at Jordan is that which enabled him not only to proclaim forgiveness and release but also to *effect* these, then this does represent a new "messianic" function of the Spirit, quite different from those envisaged by Menzies under the term *Spirit of prophecy*. This is because, for Menzies, the function of the Spirit on the predicted messiah was merely to give wisdom for sound judgment and effective rule.[130] It will become apparent in the discussion below that Menzies'

125. Menzies, *Development*, 133; Menzies, *Empowered for Witness*, 121. Menzies' concentrated argument against seeing a change in function of the Spirit at Luke 3:22 (Menzies, *Development*, 132–33; Menzies, *Empowered for Witness*, 119–21) is aimed at the work of W. B. Tatum, whose view differs somewhat from that of Dunn.

126. Menzies, *Development*, 161; Menzies, *Empowered for Witness*, 139. Menzies also notes the repeated use of *epi* ("upon") at Luke 3:22 and Luke 4:18.

127. See above, and Ervin, *Conversion-Initiation*, 18.

128. Menzies, *Development*, 166–73; Menzies, *Empowered for Witness*, 148–54.

129. Turner, "Luke and the Spirit," 61–62, 67.

130. Menzies, *Development*, 72–73; Menzies, *Empowered for Witness*, 66. Menzies probably does not do justice to *1 En.* 62:2 in making this claim. As Schweizer points

views of both Jewish and Lukan pneumatology require some modifica-
tion. At this stage, what is apparent is that Menzies has not successfully
challenged Dunn's view of Lukan salvation history as portraying three
pneumatological epochs. In that case, Jordan may be more significant, in
terms of the arrival of the new messianic age, than Menzies allows.

Pentecost: Entrance to the New Covenant?

As Menzies sees it, Dunn's claim that the gift of the Spirit granted at
Pentecost mediated the new covenant to its recipients is based squarely
on two pieces of evidence: Luke's repeated use, in this context, of *epangelia* ("promise") and the contemporary association in Jewish eyes between
the feast of Pentecost and the giving of the law to Moses at Sinai.[131] In
his discussion of the term *epangelia*, Menzies mirrors the arguments of
Ervin, adding the points that, for Luke, the promise was primarily made
in Joel 2:28–32a, and that the content of the promise was broadened at
Acts 2:39 to include both salvation (Joel 2:32a) and the Spirit of prophecy (Joel 2:28).[132]

For Menzies, Luke's use of Joel 2:28–32a at Acts 2:17–21 is most
important, for Luke himself[133] altered the wording in order to highlight
two facts: the promised gift actually presupposed salvation; and this
gift was precisely the Spirit of prophecy. In particular, Luke added *mou*
("my"; twice) and *kai prophēteusousin* ("and they will prophesy") to Joel
2:29 (at Acts 2:18). The former addition altered slaves, as a segment of
society who would receive the Spirit, into "my servants"—those already
within the new covenant who subsequently received the Spirit.[134] The
latter alteration highlighted the result of the gift: prophecy.[135] This is

---

out, the Spirit enables the Messiah "to destroy all sinners" (Schweizer, *Holy Spirit*, 41.
Schweizer warns of possible interpolation here).

131. Menzies, *Development*, 33; Menzies, *Empowered for Witness*, 32.

132. Menzies, *Development*, 200–4, 246; Menzies, *Empowered for Witness*, 168–72;
Menzies, "Luke's Understanding," 118–19.

133. Menzies, *Development*, 215–24; Menzies, *Empowered for Witness*, 178–86.

134. Compare Ervin's brief comments in Ervin, *Conversion-Initiation*, 2, 70. Menzies
notes that some manuscripts of the LXX include *mou* ("my") in Joel 2:29, but that textual criticism identifies these as later additions, probably by assimilation from Acts 2:18
(Menzies, *Development*, 220–21; cf. 216).

135. Against the suggestion that the repetition of *kai prophēteusousin* ("and they
will prophesy") represents a scribal error in Luke's source, Menzies notes not only Luke's
theological motivation, but also his affection for repetition in Old Testament quotations,

a highly important contribution to the discussion, and one for which Menzies is to be congratulated. There is no doubt, whether the redaction was Lukan or he was content to leave a source unaltered, that here Luke declared through Peter's lips that the Spirit granted on the day of Pentecost was first and foremost for prophetic enablement,[136] and that the "all flesh" who might receive this gift were in practice restricted to those who were already God's servants. This would be understood by Peter—and Luke—as those who had already committed to follow Christ, rather than simply as Jews, for only those who followed Jesus were the new "righteous remnant" of Israel (Acts 3:23).

Concerning the possible association of Pentecost with Sinai, Menzies notes that Dunn does not argue that the thought of Sinai actually determined the shape of Luke's account.[137] The question is therefore more limited and indirect: did Luke and his readers think of the Spirit's coming as a new Sinai, bringing a new covenant, *simply because this event happened at Pentecost*? The answer to this question depends on one given to a prior question: while all scholars would agree that for Jews Pentecost became a feast commemorating Sinai at some point, the question is whether this transition had already occurred by the time Luke wrote. Dunn answers, "Yes, it had," and Menzies, "No, it had not." Both agree that the fall of the Jerusalem temple to Rome in AD 70 would mark the obvious transition between Pentecost's being a harvest feast and its being a covenant festival, and that Pentecost had by that time already been associated with covenant renewal "in some sectarian circles."[138] However, while Dunn conjectures that "it is unlikely that the Rabbis after AD 70 created a new significance for Pentecost *de novo*; they doubtless took over a tradition of some antiquity and respectability,"[139] Menzies offers "decisive proof" from rabbinic literature that the association of the law with Pentecost was still a matter of dispute in the second century

---

e.g., the repetition of *apostellō* ("send"), *aphesis* ("release") and *kērussō* ("proclaim") in Luke 4:18–19 (Menzies, *Development*, 221; Menzies, *Empowered for Witness*, 184).

136. Dunn acknowledges this as a probable Lukan change highlighting prophecy (Dunn, *Acts*, 28–29).

137. Menzies, *Development*, 241 n. 2; Dunn, *Baptism*, 49.

138. Menzies, *Development*, 234; Menzies, *Empowered for Witness*, 192 (*Jub.*; Qumran literature).

139. Dunn, *Baptism*, 49.

AD.[140] In view of the difficulty in dating Luke-Acts,[141] the most help-ful answer to the question might be, "We do not know." Nevertheless, considering the probable appeal of Luke-Acts to a Gentile more than a Jewish audience, as noted above, a possible historical connection that is not explicitly supported in the text is unlikely to have the significance Dunn attaches to it.[142]

Spirit Reception: Start of a New Life?

In his study of events subsequent to Pentecost, Menzies follows other Pentecostals in rejecting Dunn's identification of reception of the Spirit with conversion. His exegesis of the Samaritan conversion covers the same points, largely, as that of Ervin. His account of Paul's experience does not engage with Dunn's. However, the Cornelius episode calls forth a response. Dunn uses the similarities between both Acts 11:17 and 18 and Acts 15:8 and 9 as evidence that by "giving Cornelius the Spirit God himself accepted Cornelius." Dunn calls the expression in Acts 11:18b the "equivalent" of that in Acts 11:17a, and calls Acts 15:9 a "synonym" of Acts 15:8.[143] In contrast, Menzies correctly identifies, in both cases, the evident reception of the Spirit as the evidential premise upon which the deduction, that Cornelius et al. were forgiven, could be based.[144] This observation builds on and develops Turner's earlier contribution.[145]

In the case of the Ephesian twelve in Acts 19:1–7, Menzies offers a fresh argument, as well as presenting several of those expressed by Dunn's

140. Menzies, *Development*, 235; Menzies, *Empowered for Witness*, 192.

141. Menzies suggests the "relatively early date" of AD 70–80 (Menzies, *Development*, 279). While O'Neill (O'Neill, *Theology of Acts*, 21, 26) dates Luke-Acts between AD 115 and 130, the consensus places the works between AD 64 and 90.

142. Turner is impressed by linguistic parallels between the account of the descent of the Spirit in Acts 2 and the account of the giving of the law at Sinai in the writings of Philo (Turner, *Power from on High*, 283–85). It is difficult to know what if any rhetorical effect might have been intended by Luke through such similarity. Given his education, Luke may have read Philo, but whether he would expect all his audience to share such a familiarity seems less likely. In contrast to Turner, Levison lists the differences between Sinai and Pentecost (Levison, *Filled with the Spirit*, 325), while for Dunn, Philo's "possible points of contact with Acts 2 are minimal" (Dunn, "Pentecost," 212).

143. Dunn, *Baptism*, 81, and n. 7. Cf. Dunn, "Baptism: A Response," 230: the Spirit is "the embodiment or transmitter of forgiveness."

144. Menzies, *Development*, 266–67; Menzies, *Empowered for Witness*, 216–17.

145. As Menzies acknowledges (Menzies, *Empowered for Witness*, 216 n. 4), his observation also rests on the earlier work of Haya-Prats, *Empowered Believers*, ch. 6.

other respondents. Menzies is emphatic that the Ephesian disciples were viewed by Luke as already Christian before they encountered Paul, not only, with Stronstad, because Luke called them *mathētas* ("disciples"), but also because they were converts of Apollos, who was clearly portrayed by Luke as a Christian (Acts 18:25). Menzies' evidence for this connection with Apollos is not convincing. Admittedly, they all knew only John's baptism (Acts 18:25; 19:3). But when Menzies writes, "Luke has carefully constructed the narrative in order to emphasize the relationship between Apollos and the Ephesians (cf. 19.1),"[146] he is surely exaggerating. Acts 19:1 hardly hints at, let alone emphasizes, such a relationship.[147] This supposed connection forces Menzies to some unlikely conclusions: Apollos was a Spirit-filled preacher (Acts 18:25); yet his converts had not heard about the Spirit (Acts 19:2); Apollos taught accurately about Jesus (Acts 18:25); Paul, nevertheless, had to teach Apollos' converts about Jesus (Acts 19:4).[148] This shaky foundation is used to support Menzies' conclusion, against Dunn, that "Luke separates the conversion (forgiveness granted in response to faith) of the twelve Ephesians from their reception of the Spirit."[149]

Conclusion

Menzies' challenge to Dunn's exegesis is of mixed quality. His understanding of the significance of Luke 1–2 and Luke 4:18–19 and his forced exegesis of Acts 18:24—19:7 do not serve well to undermine Dunn's hypothesis. However, he is considerably more impressive in his handling of the Pentecost narrative, especially the citation of Joel's prophecy, and of Cornelius' conversion and its explanation. In his study of these passages he seriously weakens Dunn's case.

MAX TURNER, 1996

The ways in which Turner in 1996 differs from Turner in 1980 are significant. Two particular instances are explicit enough to warrant mention here. One relates to a particular passage in Acts and the other to Turner's

146. Menzies, *Development*, 272; Menzies, *Empowered for Witness*, 221.

147. Bruce writes of the disciples, "how and where they received instruction must be a matter of speculation" (Bruce, *Acts*, 406); cf. Dunn, *Acts*, 254.

148. Menzies, *Development*, 272, 274; Menzies, *Empowered for Witness*, 221, 223.

149. Menzies, *Development*, 275–76; Menzies, *Empowered for Witness*, 224.

overall reading of Acts; in both cases the change serves to draw Turner in 1996 closer to Dunn than he was in 1980. The first change is that Turner now concludes from the conversion of Cornelius that his reception of the Spirit did in effect "amount to" his salvation. The second is that in Turner's later opinion reception of the Spirit was soteriologically necessary throughout Acts, even if it was not the means by which God actually granted new covenant life.

The Cornelius Episode

Turner continues to maintain against Dunn, and can now draw upon Menzies' work for support, that Acts 11:17–18 and 15:8–9 do not render as synonymous "giving the Holy Spirit to them" and "cleansing their hearts by faith" (taking Acts 15:8–9 as an example).[150] However, the overall picture created by the three records of Cornelius' conversion in Acts 10:1–48, 11:4–17, and 15:7–9 leads him to conclude that "the Spirit manifest in them [Cornelius' household] is the very power by which the Messiah purges 'Israel.'" Therefore, "Dunn's reading was actually along the right lines: the Spirit of prophecy is simultaneously the soteriological Spirit."[151] Turner reaches this conclusion by noticing the repetition, for the first time since Acts 1, of the phrase "baptized with the Holy Spirit" and the recollection of John the Baptist's ministry in Acts 11:16. For Turner in 1996 as in 1980 (see above), the Baptist's promise of a Coming One who would baptize with the Spirit could not mean that this Coming One would actually grant the Spirit to others, for pre-Christian Judaism had no concept of anyone except God granting God's Spirit (and the Coming One was definitely human: he would wear sandals). Rather, the Spirit upon the Coming One would be the means whereby he would cleanse Israel: there would be a purging with Spirit-and-fire for all Israel through Jesus' ministry. Therefore the remembered promise in Acts 11:16 is that the Messiah would purge and thereby restore Israel by this Spirit. Just as the arrival of the Spirit in Cornelius' household indicated that these Gentiles had now been accepted by God into "Israel," so too it indicated that they were part of the purged Israel—and it must have been the Spirit who had purged them.[152]

150. Turner, *Power from on High*, 382–84.
151. Ibid., 387.
152. Ibid., 387, drawing on his arguments earlier presented on pp. 177–87.

Turner's argumentation at this point displays several weaknesses. First, whether or not other pre-Christian Judaism conceived of a coming messiah who would himself grant the Spirit of God, Luke portrayed John the Baptist as an extraordinary prophet (Luke 1:15–17, 76; 3:2; 7:26). One must allow that God might have revealed this theological novelty to John—and that Luke would have understood the course of events thus.[153] Secondly, Turner's repeated insistence that in John's understanding to be baptized with the Spirit was to be purged or cleansed is questionable. Because Luke 3:16 has *en pneumati hagiō kai puri* ("with the Holy Spirit and fire") rather than "with the Holy Spirit and *with* fire," Turner too readily follows Dunn in inferring that the promise is for "Spirit-and-fire": one common experience of fiery Spirit as the lot of all recipients, albeit experienced as blessing by the repentant and as judgement by the unrepentant.[154] However, Luke 3:17 indicates that fire would be reserved solely for the chaff, and Luke 3:9, in another metaphor, that fire would only be for those trees that did not bear good fruit (the fruit worthy of repentance specifically—Luke 3:8). One might conclude that John's audience, divided by whether or not each individual would submit to his baptism (Luke 3:3, 7–17; 7:29–30), would be divided in days to come between those who would receive the Spirit and those who would receive the fire.[155] This fire would then be for judgement (destruction, not purging).[156]

153. So Dunn, "Spirit-and-Fire Baptism," 102.

154. Dunn, *Baptism*, 11; Dunn, "Spirit-and-Fire Baptism," 95; Turner, *Power from on High*, 177–79, 405, 421, etc. Admittedly, in *Holy Spirit and Spiritual Gifts*, Turner writes that "Holy Spirit and fire" is only "probably" a hendiadys (ibid., 25).

155. Dunn, *Baptism* 11 n. 10, weakens his own case for a single fiery Spirit baptism with the observation that the "you" addressed by John in Luke 3:16 are probably not solely those who were baptized. As he notes, John was speaking generally to the crowds, who included both those submitting to baptism and those refusing it (Luke 3:7; 7:30). Therefore, he addressed a divided audience.

156. As presented by Luke, John the Baptist, prophetically endowed, expected an exalted messiah. This great prophet John, filled with the Spirit, able to command the attention of crowds of Jews *and* soldiers, able to rebuke a king, able to persuade masses to engage in an unprecedented rite, expected a Coming One of whom he, John, was not worthy even to be a *slave*. The very fact that John was himself mistaken by the crowds for the awaited Messiah heightens the exaltation of his expected "Coming One" yet further: John, so significant in his hearers' opinion that he himself might be the Messiah, is less than a slave before a master compared to the One who will come. John merely separated Israel, through the "winnowing" process of Spirit-inspired, prophetic, challenging, ethical preaching and teaching. His Coming One would reward or judge the separated parties: the fire of destructive judgement would be for the unrepentant;

So for what purpose would the Spirit be given? With a few exceptions, Jews probably did not expect the eschatological outpouring of the Spirit upon all God's people to purge or cleanse them.[157] Israel was already cleansed through its Exodus from its slavery to foreign dominion into the blessing of God's rule, and kept clean by the gracious provisions of the covenant that God had given. Not even the Old Testament passage that most closely juxtaposed thoughts of the Spirit's future arrival to all Israelites with their future cleansing (Ezek 36) stated that the coming Spirit would actually do the cleansing. Rather, the cleansing would be achieved by the agency of water (albeit perhaps to be understood metaphorically) and the Spirit would subsequently move the cleansed Israelites to keep God's laws, so as not to soil themselves once again (Ezek 36:25–29a).[158] So the antecedent expectations of John's hearers would not bring cleansing to

the reward of a place in the granary would be for the repentant remnant. On this basis, to be immersed or engulfed in the Spirit looks like a reward for those already "cleansed" by their separation from the chaff through a repentant response to John's preaching (a cleansing already symbolized in John's baptism). Similarly, Stronstad, *Baptized and Filled*, 56, 59; Stronstad, "On Being Baptized," 165.

157. Certainly, as Turner notes with reference to Isa 11:1–4; *1 En.* 62:2; *Pss. Sol.* 18:7; *4 Ezra* 13:8–11; 1QSb 5:24–25; etc., the anointed Messiah was expected to exercise judgement and thereby purge Israel. However, this purging purpose did not usually extend to expectations of the wider eschatological outpouring on Israel as a whole. Thus Isa 4:4 probably refers to the work of the Spirit in and through the Branch of 4:2 (cf. Isa 11:1–4). Dunn also refers in this context to *Jub.* 1:23 and 1QS 4:21. *Jub.* 1:23 does admittedly state that "after this they will return to me in all uprightness and with all of (their) heart and soul. And I shall cut off the foreskin of their heart . . . And I shall create for them a holy spirit, and I shall purify them so that they will not turn away from following me" (translation from Charlesworth, *Pseudepigrapha Vol. 2*, 54). 1QS 4:21 declares that God, "will cleanse him of all wicked deeds with the spirit of holiness; like purifying waters He will shed upon him the spirit of truth (to cleanse him) of all abomination and injustice. And he shall be plunged into the spirit of purification" (translation from Vermes, *Complete Dead Sea Scrolls*, 103). The context immediately before this passage might suggest that the object of this purifying is humanity in general ("children of men"—1QS 4:15). However, the following words are: "that he may instruct the upright in the knowledge of the Most High and teach the wisdom of the sons of heaven to the perfect of way." Thus it is unclear whether the passage refers to humanity in general, or to a specific teacher, as the recipient of the cleansing spirit.

158. So Menzies, "Luke's Understanding," 119. Turner discusses how this passage was understood—in combination with Joel 2:28—in later rabbinic literature. While the literature in question dates from AD 200 to 500, it may be the product of older traditions that have some bearing on interpretation of the New Testament. In this rabbinic understanding, the Spirit of prophecy would enable recipients to know God's will, and thereby implicitly obey this will, but did not cleanse them in the first place (Turner, *Power from on High*, 130–31; cf. Menzies, *Empowered for Witness*, 95–96).

their minds when they heard his promise expressed. Only the physical act of John's own baptism in water might do that. However, that baptism was as likely to speak to their imaginations of deluge or flood as it was to speak of cleansing.[159] Such "liquid metaphors" were to be found in Old Testament texts that associated the coming Spirit with rain on thirsty ground, not to cleanse the ground but to bring fresh life and growth (Isa 32:15; 44:3; Ezek 39:29; Joel 2:28 [cf. 2:23]). The hope for John's hearers would then be that God's Spirit, granted anew by the Messiah, would bring new life, growth, and activity. Turner's association with cleansing, of which connection he makes much in the logic of his later arguments such as over Acts 11:16–18, is questionable.

To return now to the account of Cornelius and his associates, the significance of their reception of the Spirit must be gleaned from more immediate markers than how John the Baptist's promises might have been remembered and understood. Clearly, the recipients were enabled to engage in charismatic praise (Acts 10:46). It is valid to imagine that there was an inner psychological/spiritual corollary to this outward behavior: this is certainly the conclusion to which those who heard them at the time immediately leaped. Thus the greatest significance, in the flow of Luke's narrative, was the sign value that this outburst of praise had for the listeners. For these somewhat skeptical Jews, this was the divine attestation that God had done an "inner" work, even in Gentiles. The arrival of the Spirit did not itself cleanse the recipients' hearts. Rather, it simply *indicated* in an undeniably divine way (to their thinking) that *God* had cleansed their hearts.

The Soteriological Spirit

Turner's second alteration to his 1980 view, that drawn from the general picture in Acts, can be expressed straightforwardly and briefly: once Jesus had been withdrawn from the disciples' physical presence through the ascension, the only means by which those disciples and all who followed could experience the presence of Jesus, and indeed the presence

159. As both Dunn (Dunn, "Baptism Yet Once More," 14) and Turner (Turner, *Power from on High*, 181) observe, there was a Jewish expectation of an eschatological river of fire that would destroy the wicked, and that this was to emanate from the coming Messiah. Given that there was an expectation of an eschatological river of water that would bring life (Ezek 47), it is not unreasonable to imagine that John, Spirit-filled prophet that he was, might have also expected this river to flow from the Coming One.

of God, was by the Holy Spirit.[160] Therefore, without the physical presence of Jesus, though people might gain indirect, mediated experiences of the Spirit through the preaching or other ministries of those who were already endowed, Christian life could only be experienced in any meaningful ongoing sense through receiving the gift of the Spirit for oneself. As salvation in Luke was more than merely crossing some line from "unforgiven" to "forgiven,"[161] but was incorporation into a community that was existentially experiencing the life of the kingdom of God, as mediated through the words and works of Jesus, it is no exaggeration to call the Spirit *soteriologically necessary*, or, more briefly, to refer to the "soteriological Spirit." Thus, Turner notes toward the end of *Power from on High* that he finds "the evidence partially supporting Dunn's position, even if we have arrived there by different arguments."[162]

Turner's change of opinion from his 1980 position has come about through his increased attention to the simple observation that, notwithstanding the exception of the Samaritan episode in Acts 8, Acts 2:38 stands as programmatic for all of Acts and announces that the norm to be expected in all cases of conversion to the gospel is that the Spirit will be received, to quote Turner, as "part and parcel" of the experience.[163] If, he has asked himself, Luke only regarded the gift of the Spirit as necessary for mission, why was this gift so tightly bound up with Christian beginnings?[164] One might otherwise expect, he speculates, the Acts 8 picture to be the norm, and converts to receive training over a period of time before they are ready to receive the Spirit who will now empower them to go out on the mission they have learnt to engage in.[165] Further evidence, for Turner, lies in the absence of any record in Acts of the whole Christian community engaging in evangelistic outreach. This, Turner asserts, is reserved for relatively few especially endowed individuals.[166]

---

160. Turner, *Power from on High*, e.g., 358, 435, 438.

161. Turner critiques a "low" view of Lukan salvation among Pentecostals in Turner, *Power from on High*, 346, 422, 436.

162. Ibid., 437.

163. Ibid., especially 352–60; quotation from 398.

164. Ibid., e.g., 360, 437.

165. Ibid., 360.

166. E.g., Turner, *Power from on High*, 398, Turner, *Holy Spirit and Spiritual Gifts*, 47. He repeats this point emphatically in dialogue with Stronstad, in Turner, "Does Luke Believe Reception of the Spirit makes all 'Prophets'?"

The majority are merely an audience for the activities of the apostles and other unusually gifted individuals. Therefore, the Spirit must be given for a purpose that is necessary for all believers, not just evangelists, and is necessary from the very inception of Christian life: this purpose must be the granting of subjective experience of Jesus to those receiving the Spirit.

Whether Turner is correct in asserting that the gift of the Spirit is necessary, after the ascension, for people to experience Jesus directly is a question that will require detailed response. I shall thus return to that matter in the next chapter. At this stage, I want to respond to the other aspects of his argument here: the connection of the gift of the Spirit to Christian beginnings (which is indeed programmatically announced at Acts 2:38) and the absence of evidence for evangelism conducted by the wider Christian populace. Turner's observations at this point suffer a weakness: he seems to make unwarranted assumptions about the church Luke presented. Luke may have been relatively quiet about the evangelistic activities of believers in general (though note Acts 8:1–4; 11:19–21) and it is true that Luke's summary passages (Acts 2:42–47; 4:32–35) do not mention outreach among the many activities of the "ordinary" believers that are mentioned. Nevertheless, the likely activities of these people must be judged partly by what Jesus had earlier promised: if Acts 2:38 is programmatic for the ideal timing of Spirit reception in Christian conversion, Acts 1:8 is equally programmatic for the role of the Spirit in a believer's life.[167] It will not suffice to argue that the words recorded in Acts 1:8 were addressed by Jesus only to his immediate disciples or only to the church in general rather than to the individuals within it.[168]

167. Turner himself repeatedly refers to Luke 24:49 and Acts 1:8 as "gateway redactional texts" (Turner, *Holy Spirit and Spiritual Gifts*, 38, 53; Turner, "'Spirit of Prophecy' as the Power of Israel's Restoration," 330, 345). One would expect him to suggest by the term "gateway" that Acts 1:8 is the only "means of entry" to Acts, and that its whole narrative should be read in this light. However, Turner does not grant as much weight to Acts 1:8 in his exegesis of the later narrative as he does to Acts 2:38, which text and its context he regards as "normative" and "genuinely programmatic" (Turner, *Power from on High*, 352; cf. 392: "norm"). Thus at this point Turner is vulnerable to the same criticism that Petts levels at Dunn: Acts 1:8 is relatively ignored. As Penney observes with reference to Dunn, "If . . . the Spirit is the *sine qua non* of being a Christian, then one must also assert that mission is the *sine qua non* of Christian activity" (Penney, *Missionary Emphasis*, 109).

168. Turner, *Power from on High*, 399. Neither will it suffice to argue that Acts 1:8 is prominent merely because mission is an important theme in Luke's writing (Turner,

For Luke, these words were clearly fulfilled in the events noted in Acts 2:4, and this filling was certainly for all the 120 individuals referred to in Acts 1:15. Furthermore, while only Peter preached the sermon on the day of Pentecost, all the 120 spoke, in foreign tongues, of the greatness of God. It was this multilingual declaration of God's greatness that first attracted the crowd to hear Peter's sermon. Luke highlighted, perhaps deliberately, a link between the words of the 120 and the words of Peter by using the same verb, *apophthengesthai* ("to declare"), of both (Acts 2:4, 14).[169] Thus a form of spontaneous and humanly unintended teamwork between the 120 and the single preacher is evident. That the promise of Acts 1:8 was viewed by Luke as a general promise for all is confirmed later in Acts by God's answer to prayer recorded in Acts 4:31. All the gathered believers on that occasion were filled with the Spirit and spoke God's word boldly. That this was not a conversion-initiation context does not matter. To argue that this group was a gathering of Peter and John's friends, and so somehow did not represent the generality of Christian believers, is a frank case of special pleading.[170] In summary, Luke's overall portrayal is of a church in which all were engaged in active witness (while no doubt some of these witnesses had as much prominence in the task as the record of their exploits has prominence in the text of Acts). According to Luke 24:49, and the whole implicit tenor of Acts, this engagement in witness required the help of God's Spirit, given to the believing heart. It is no surprise, then, that this gift was presented as available from, and ideally received in the process of, conversion-initiation. Only thus might all converts to Christ be empowered for their active participation in the mission of Christ's church from the start of their Christian lives.

Holy Spirit and Spiritual Gifts, 47). Such circular argumentation begs the question: if Luke stressed worldwide mission, and if he emphatically linked this with Spirit reception, then is not a reader who disentangles these twin themes (at least in the lives of "ordinary" believers) in danger of misrepresenting Luke and his concerns?

169. See discussion in Levison, *Filled with the Spirit*, 358.

170. Turner, *Power from on High*, 359, 399; Turner, *Holy Spirit and Spiritual Gifts*, 47. Special pleading is evident elsewhere. I quote in full: "Acts 8:1 generalises that 'all' were scattered, and 8:4 that 'those who were scattered went about preaching the word,' but the latter does not repeat the 'all' of 8:1, and in no way suggests that 'each' preached the word; merely that, as a result of their going out, the word was spread (by some)" (Turner, "'Spirit of Prophecy' as the Power of Israel's Restoration," 341 n. 48). Turner has to admit elsewhere that "Luke may well have believed a majority of Christians became involved in different types of spoken witness" (Turner, *Holy Spirit and Spiritual Gifts*, 47). Turner should allow this admission to influence his Lukan pneumatology more profoundly.

Conclusion

In conclusion, Turner in 1996 finds himself much closer to Dunn's stance than he did in 1980, even if he does not use Dunn's logic. Fuller evaluation of Turner will need to wait to the next chapter, but it is already evident that Turner's newer position is vulnerable to significant critique, so that it may be wiser to listen to Turner's voice from 1980 as part of the Pentecostal response to be mounted against Dunn's thesis.

CONCLUSIONS

In this concluding section of the chapter, I will bring together and assess corporately the works of Dunn's Pentecostal respondents in order to answer the question: is a creditable refutation offered of Dunn's claim that in Luke's eyes to "become a Christian, in short, is to receive the Spirit of Christ, the Holy Spirit. What the Pentecostal attempts to separate into two works of God is in fact one single divine act"?[171] The next chapter will then go on to consider whether, if these debaters have indeed cast significant doubt on Dunn's thesis, they have in turn offered an adequate alternative to Dunn's position.

A review of six Lukan passages should suffice to decide whether Dunn's arguments have been adequately met.

LUKE 3:21—4:21. By pointing to Luke 4:18–21, the significance of which Dunn has seriously underestimated, Dunn's critics have correctly identified Luke's understanding of the Jordan anointing: it was essentially an empowering to minister to others. However, Dunn's contention that the Jordan marked Jesus' entry into the new age and covenant has been less well handled. Unconvincing attempts have been made to rid the Jordan event of eschatological significance. Criticism of Dunn would have been better placed focusing on his consistent linking of "new era" with "new covenant." For instance, he writes, "Only with the descent of the Spirit does the new covenant and the new epoch enter, and only thus does Jesus himself enter the new covenant and epoch."[172] While Luke would probably agree with Dunn (!) that Jesus entered a new epoch at the Jordan, it is unlikely that he would accept that Jesus "entered" the new covenant. Luke's opinion concerning Jesus' relationship to the new covenant is much more that Jesus was its agent: that he brought it to the

---

171. Dunn, *Baptism*, 96.
172. Ibid., 32.

world, than that the Spirit brought it to him. This is the implication of the fullest text of Luke 22:20,[173] as well as of Luke's probable association of Jesus with the Isaianic servant (Luke 3:22d, echoing Isa 42:1b), who was himself to be the covenant (Isa 42:6).

ACTS 1:1—2:39. Through their study of Luke's use of *epangelia* ("promise"), Dunn's respondents have successfully dissociated the gift of the Spirit to the 120 from mediation of the new covenant. Turner has traced back new covenant blessings into the lives of the disciples during Jesus' earthly ministry, while Shelton has drawn attention to the period after the ascension. Dunn is right to observe that the disciples at that time drew lots to choose a twelfth apostle. However, they worshiped Jesus (Luke 24:52[174]), called him "Lord" (Acts 1:21), and, of course, believed in his resurrection (Acts 1:22). This sounds, from Luke's viewpoint, like authentic new covenant life. Dunn's debaters have also succeeded in reflecting more faithfully than Dunn Luke's emphasis on power as that which the Spirit brings (e.g., Acts 1:4–8). Furthermore, Menzies' excellent study of the redaction of Joel 2:28–32 in Acts 2:17–21 highlights Luke's emphasis on both the prophetic nature of the Pentecostal gift and his understanding that the recipients of the gift were already God's servants (cf. Acts 5:32). However, only Petts and Turner, with Dunn, are prepared to admit the implication of Acts 2:38 that Spirit reception was in Luke's eyes a part of full Christian initiation after Pentecost.[175]

ACTS 8:4–25. This definitely represents the Pentecostals' strongest ground, and Dunn's weakest. Dunn's thesis that the Samaritans' faith was defective prior to their Spirit reception has itself been shown to be "defective." Dunn himself, as I noted in the previous chapter, has softened his position over the years concerning this vital passage, and necessarily so: the Samaritans' effective faith and accepted baptism, occurring prior to the apostles' visit, show that for Luke it was possible to be a baptized believer and yet not have the Spirit.

ACTS 9:1–19. This passage has called forth far less response. None has refuted Dunn's convincing claim that Paul's blindness could not be symbolic, for Luke, of Paul's completed conversion. Whatever steps in the

173. Various early witnesses attest to manuscript discrepancies here.

174. Admittedly, there is textual doubt here.

175. Contrast Stronstad: "In the immediate context of his own reception of the Spirit, Peter's promise of the Spirit [Acts 2:38] thus lacks any initiation/incorporation connotations" (Stronstad, *Charismatic Theology*, 69).

process had already occurred prior to Ananias' visit, it was only through Ananias' ministry to him that the scales fell from Paul's eyes, to use Luke's evocative phrase.

ACTS 10:34—11:18. The strength of the response in this case lies not in suggesting any degree of subsequence between salvation and Spirit reception, but in rebutting, successfully, Dunn's conclusion that these two divine gifts were necessarily understood by Luke as the same thing. "Being given the Spirit" was not a synonym for "being granted repentance unto life." Rather, the Spirit's arrival provided the outward evidence, to those who could not read human hearts (Acts 15:8),[176] of what God was doing within the recipient.

ACTS 19:1–7. This passage is distinctive in the variety of responses that it has stimulated. Many are not impressive. Amidst the speculative questions about the time gap between baptism and laying on of hands, and about any possible relationship between the Ephesian disciples and Apollos, one convincing point has emerged. The record of Paul's question coincided with Luke's thought: belief was possible without reception of the Spirit.

In conclusion, Dunn's Pentecostal critics have corrected two basic weaknesses in his view of Lukan pneumatology. They have brought to light a distinction in Luke's thought between (a) entrance to the new covenant through forgiveness of sin and (b) reception of the gift of the Spirit, which Luke presented rather as divine empowering for the various enterprises of the church. Also, they have made it clear that for Luke it was possible, both in historical occurrence (Acts 8:16) and apostolic thinking (Acts 19:2), to believe without having received the Spirit. The aspect of the Pentecostal response that has been much weaker has been the handling of Dunn's claim that Spirit reception was initiatory. There is a divorce in some Pentecostal thought between Christian beginnings and Spirit reception that is not Lukan.

In the next chapter, I will go on to assess the various alternatives to Dunn's thesis that his debaters have offered. While in general this allows for debate *within* Pentecostalism (as the alternatives can be compared with each other), Turner stands apart: his more recent alternatives must be considered "ex-Pentecostal."

---

176. Turner, *Power from on High*, 383–84 n. 107.

3

Pentecostal Alternatives to Dunn

INTRODUCTION

IN THE PREVIOUS CHAPTER, we saw the various ways in which the Pentecostals under review have found fault with Dunn's primary thesis and the relative strengths of their criticisms. We saw that, overall, the Pentecostal exegesis of Luke-Acts significantly questions Dunn's case. For Luke, the Pentecostal gift of the Spirit was *not* the means whereby God granted forgiveness. Neither did God necessarily grant the gift at this point in a convert's "spiritual journey." This chapter takes the question further. The Pentecostals' relative success in refuting Dunn's arguments does not automatically mean that their understanding of Lukan pneumatology is accurate. A convincing alternative to Dunn's view needs to be offered. As became apparent in the previous chapter, Pentecostals correctly understand Luke to have indicated that, rather than being the reception of new covenant life, the reception of the Spirit was a possibly later enabling or empowering for that life, or at least for certain aspects of it. But this raises three questions. First, if it was possibly subsequent to conversion, was reception of the Spirit for Luke attached to Christian initiation at all? Was it completely unrelated to Christian beginnings, or was it still somehow tied up with them? Secondly, what precisely did Luke understand the Spirit's enabling to be? What could people do after they had received the Spirit that they could not do before? Thirdly, is it possible to disagree with Dunn, but still see the Spirit's enabling as so all-encompassing that meaningful Christian life is impossible without it? We will take the first question, about initiation, now, as it can be dealt with relatively briefly, and then we will turn in detail to the second question, about empowering, before tackling Turner's answer to the third question.

SPIRIT RECEPTION AND CHRISTIAN BEGINNINGS

Disagreement amongst the Pentecostals under review has emerged over whether Luke portrayed delay between belief and Spirit baptism as normal or abnormal. Speaking of the Samaritan "delay," Stronstad writes that "such a temporal separation is typical of the outpourings of the Spirit in Acts."[1] However, Petts and Turner disagree. To quote Petts on the subject, "Luke intends us to understand the Samaritan situation as abnormal."[2]

In assessing which of these views is more accurate, it might first be noted that Petts and Turner share the opinion of other commentators.[3] Secondly, the answer does not lie in statistics. It is not enough for one to say, "The 120, Paul, the Caesareans, and the Ephesians all received the Spirit at the moment they entered the new covenant; therefore the Samaritan delay is abnormal!" or for another to declare, "The 120, Paul, and the Ephesians were all born again before receiving the Spirit; therefore the Samaritan case is normal, and that of Cornelius abnormal!" Quite apart from some of the difficulties of interpretation that these passages offer, five accounts of Spirit reception is simply not a statistically significant sample. All these five occasions reveal is that Luke was well aware of variety in timing.[4]

Other pointers must be sought. First, is there any clue in the Samaritan account itself that shows us Luke's opinion of its normality? Turner responds in the affirmative: Luke had to supply an "awkward 'explanation'" in Acts 8:16.[5] It is difficult to detect any awkwardness about this explanation, but Turner probably has a point, given that the explanation is there at all. Turner's stronger basis for his view, that Acts 8

---

1. Stronstad, *Charismatic Theology*, 65.

2. Petts, "Baptism in the Holy Spirit," 65; similarly Turner, "Luke and the Spirit," 162; Turner, *Power from on High*, 360. Also in agreement, without specific reference to Luke-Acts, is Dye, "Are Pentecostals Pentecostal?" 24–25.

3. See Lampe, *Seal of the Spirit*, 70; Green, *I Believe in the Holy Spirit*, 139; Smail, *Reflected Glory*, 145; Penney, *Missionary Emphasis*, 107.

4. Compare Hunter, *Spirit Baptism*, 90: "The 'pattern' in Acts is the absence of uniformity in sequence." Also Witherington, *Acts*, 289.

5. Turner, "Luke and the Spirit," 162; also Bruner, *Theology of the Holy Spirit*, 177–78.

represents abnormality, is Luke's presentation of authoritative apostolic teaching on the subject.[6] While Luke believed that in apostolic thought a believer might not yet have the Spirit (Acts 19:2), he presented, programmatically, an apostolic promise that people would receive the Spirit at initiation (Acts 2:38): "The natural understanding of Acts 2:38–39 would be that as a rule of thumb the Spirit will from now on be given by God to those who repent and are baptized, without further conditions (for none is specified) and without delay (for none is implied)."[7] Turner plausibly offers the normality of this pattern, in Luke's mind, as the reason for the absence of references to Spirit reception in so many of Luke's later accounts of people's conversions.[8] Also, he makes the excellent point that Paul in conversation with the Ephesian disciples of Acts 19:1–6 followed up their admission that they did not know of the Spirit with the question, "Into what then were you baptized?" (Acts 19:3), thereby indicating that in the Lukan Paul's mind Spirit reception was linked, typically, with baptismal initiation into Christian discipleship.[9]

In conclusion, those Pentecostal arguments that wrest baptism in the Spirit entirely from Christian beginnings do not accurately represent Lukan pneumatology. As Turner observes, Luke presented a believer (or apparent believer) without the Spirit as an anomaly, an anomaly that called for an immediate corrective response from the church (Acts 8:15; 19:2–6).[10] If Spirit reception was thus a part of Christian beginnings, does that mean, with Dunn, that for Luke one could not be a Christian at all without the Spirit? Petts is able to say, "One could."[11] He does this

---

6. In the debate concerning the possible priority of Pauline teaching over Lukan history for forming a New Testament pneumatology (see, e.g., Stronstad, *Charismatic Theology*, 5–9; Fee, *Gospel and Spirit*, ch. 6) we must not overlook that Luke deliberately portrayed authoritative teaching through the speeches and conversations of, especially, the apostles.

7. Turner, *Power from on High*, 358. Menzies comes close to, but falls short of, agreeing: "While the collocation [in Acts 2:38] may indicate that for Luke the rite of water baptism is normally accompanied by the bestowal of the Spirit, Luke's usage elsewhere suggests that even this conclusion may be overstating the case . . . the most that can be gleaned from the text is that repentance and water baptism are the normal prerequisites for reception of the Spirit, which is promised to very believer" (Menzies, "Luke's Understanding," 120).

8. Turner, *Power from on High*, 359; similarly Twelftree, *People of the Spirit*, 96, 99.

9. Turner, *Power from on High*, 392.

10. Ibid., 398.

11. Petts, "Baptism in the Holy Spirit," 60, 66.

by supplying his own definition of a Christian: the Samaritan incident "shows it to be possible to be a Christian (in the sense of having genuinely believed and been baptized) and yet not to have received the Spirit."[12] Petts' definition may be common, but was it Luke's? It *probably* was. Luke only used the term *Christian* twice, so the data on which we can draw is sparse. Nonetheless, in Acts 11:26 he collocated it with the word *disciple*, and the terms here do appear to be synonyms (though bear in mind the arguments over Acts 19:2!). It is perhaps safest to say, by arguing from Luke's silence, that Luke knew of no *long-term ongoing* Christianity without reception of the Spirit. However, to judge that ongoing Christianity without the Spirit might be impossible is not the same thing as judging that early discipleship without the Spirit was impossible. To repeat: Luke declared that in authoritative apostolic experience (that of Peter and John) a convert could be validly baptized in water as such and not yet have received the Spirit (Acts 8) and that in authoritative apostolic thinking (that of Paul) the question could be posed whether someone, coming to belief, had yet received the Spirit (Acts 19:2). What part the Spirit might have played in those earliest stages of coming to belief is a matter that will gain our attention later in the chapter, when Turner's thesis is explored in more depth.

PENTECOSTAL ENABLING

Dunn's respondents are unanimous: Luke portrayed Spirit reception not as the receiving of new covenant life and forgiveness from sin, but as a powerful enabling. But what precisely is this enabling, and what is it for? "Power-in-mission" is the term frequently used by Ervin, but he does not define or describe the concept that lies behind it.[13] Petts refers to "power for service," but offers no information on its nature. Stronstad, Shelton, Menzies, and Turner, though less uniform in their terminology, are more expansive in their descriptions. I will thus study them in turn, and again in chronological order, with primary reference to Turner at this stage being to his 1996 work. For this reason, I will consider him after Menzies.

---

12. Ibid., 66.

13. Power for the missionary enterprise is also highlighted by, among others, Arrington, *Acts of the Apostles*, xxxvii–xl; Congar, *I Believe in the Holy Spirit*, 44–47; Keener, "Spirit-Filled Teaching," 46–47; Lampe, *Seal of the Spirit*, 72–73; Marshall, *Luke: Historian and Theologian*, 199–201; Michaels, "Luke-Acts"; Penney, *Missionary Emphasis*; and Warrington, *Message of the Holy Spirit*, ch. 10.

Stronstad and Shelton can be considered together, for there is not much difference between them on this point.

Enabling in What Sense?—Stronstad and Shelton

Stronstad understands Luke's pneumatology to be in continuity with that suggested by "charismatic" material in the Old Testament. The only differences are that for Luke "the vocational activity of the Spirit is now potentially universal," "its new object is the ongoing mission of the Messiah," and "the Holy Spirit is fully personal."[14] Otherwise, Luke's concept accurately reflects the Old Testament view of the Spirit's charismatic activity.[15] This activity he defines: "By 'charismatic' I mean God's gift of His Spirit to His servants, either individually or collectively, to anoint, empower, or inspire them for divine service. As it is recorded in Scripture, therefore, this charismatic activity is necessarily an experiential phenomenon."[16] Stronstad finds three charismatic motifs that he believes shape Lukan pneumatology.

> a. The "transfer motif."[17] When Old Testament leadership responsibility was transferred to a new person, so was the necessary endowment of the Spirit. Examples are the transfer from Moses to the elders (Num 11:10–30), from Moses to Joshua (Deut 34:9), from Saul to David (1 Sam 16:13–14), and from Elijah to Elisha (2 Kgs 2:9). Stronstad sees this motif paralleled in the Lukan "transfer" of the Spirit from Jesus to the disciples at Pentecost (Acts 2:33).[18]
>
> b. The "sign motif."[19] When the Spirit came on a character prophecy was often the initial result (Num 11:25; 1 Chr 12:18; 2 Chr 15:1; 20:14–15; 24:20; Ezek 11:5). On some occasions at least, this prophecy served as a sign of God's anointing, both to the recipient (1 Sam 10:6–7) and to observers (1 Sam 10:9–11).

---

14. Stronstad, *Charismatic Theology*, 79.
15. Ibid., 13, 32.
16. Ibid., 13.
17. Ibid., 20–21; Stronstad, *Baptized and Filled*, 14–15.
18. Stronstad, *Charismatic Theology*, 49.
19. Ibid., 21–22; Stronstad, *Baptized and Filled*, 15.

For Stronstad, this motif was reflected in the tongues or prophecy that accompanied Lukan Spirit receptions.[20]

c. The "vocational motif."[21] When the charismatic activity of the
Spirit was evident in the Old Testament, the recipient was
equipped for a particular task. Thus the Spirit granted wisdom
to the builders of the tabernacle (Exod 31:3, LXX), understanding to Joshua (Deut 34:9, LXX), military ability to Othniel
(Judg 3:10), and physical strength to Samson (Judg 14:6). So,
too, notes Stronstad, the Lukan gift of the Spirit was vocational,
empowering Christian ministry.[22]

Is Stronstad's choice of Old Testament charismatic pneumatology as a background against which to view Luke's words valid? Against
Stronstad, it might be asked why Luke should have chosen to portray
only the Spirit's charismatic activity, when the Old Testament also witnesses, albeit less frequently, to creative (Gen 1:2 [possibly]; Job 33:4; Ps
33:6), ethical (Ps 51:11, LXX; Isa 63:10), rational (Neh 9:20; Job 32:8),
and life-giving (Ezek 37:1–14) activities.[23] Also, Stronstad's contention
that Luke's dependence upon Old Testament charismatic pneumatology
is not only conceptual but also terminological is exaggerated. Stronstad
repeatedly refers to Luke's indebtedness to the Septuagint for terms to
denote the Spirit's reception and activities.[24] Yet Luke's two favorite verbs
in this range (*pimplēmi* ["fill"], and *lambanō* ["receive"]) are not found
in the Septuagint with *pneuma* ("S/spirit").[25] Thirdly, it has become apparent through study of Menzies' and Turner's investigations that the
Old Testament's concepts of the Spirit had evolved significantly by the
time they were communicated to Luke by the early hellenistic-Jewish
Christianity of which he was an heir. A more likely explanation than

20. E.g., Stronstad, *Charismatic Theology*, 79.

21. Ibid., 23–24; Stronstad, *Baptized and Filled*, 13–14.

22. Stronstad, *Charismatic Theology*, 77–78.

23. See Montague, *Holy Spirit*, 48–49, 74–76; Schweizer, *Holy Spirit*, 15–16, 20–21;
Hill, *Greek Words*, 210–12.

24. Stronstad, *Charismatic Theology*, 13, 50, 52, 61, 76, 77; Stronstad, *Baptized and
Filled*, 17–18, 75–78.

25. Luke's language in this context is as similar to Paul's as it is to the Septuagint. See
the table in my "Pentecostal Responses: Luke-Acts," 130–31. Admittedly, the LXX does
occasionally use *empimplēmi*. The three commonest LXX verbs in this context are not
found in Luke-Acts.

Stronstad's for his finding similarities in the Old Testament is that
Stronstad has read Luke's pneumatology back into certain Old Testament
passages that seem especially amenable.

Despite these criticisms, Stronstad's exegesis of Luke's own works
is largely accurate. Stronstad repeatedly describes the gift of the Spirit as
"charismatic" and the concept covered is suitably broad: it is an experienced equipping for any task to which an individual or group is called.[26]
This equipping is presented as including:

a.   *Power.* By this Stronstad means the ability to perform miracles
     and the ability to witness persuasively (Acts 2:41) and boldly
     (Acts 4:31).[27]

b.   *Prophecy.* By this, Stronstad refers to "invasive" speeches of
     worship, witness, and judgement (Acts 2:4; 4:8–12; 13:11) and
     to guidance given through visions and dreams (Acts 10:19;
     16:9).[28]

c.   *Wisdom and faith.* Stronstad connects these qualities with the
     Spirit on the basis of Acts 6:3, 5; 11:24.[29]

Stronstad's broad concept of the Spirit's enablement reflects Luke's twin
concern that the church's tasks were both empowered and directed by
the Spirit.[30]

While Stronstad rightly agrees with Menzies (see below) that the
Spirit was given primarily to equip the church's missionary expansion,
he does give somewhat more recognition to the breadth of service that
the Spirit might enable, so that he can conclude, "Luke relates the gift of
the Spirit to service and witness; that is, to vocation."[31] This breadth of
view arises as much from Stronstad's understanding of the vocational
motif in the Old Testament as from his reading of Luke. Like Menzies,
he does not develop the implications that Acts 6:3, 5; 11:28; 13:52; 15:28
offer concerning the ministry of the Spirit within the church.

26. Stronstad, *Charismatic Theology*, 13.

27. Ibid., 51, 52, 55, 72.

28. Ibid., 55, 80.

29. Ibid., 55.

30. See especially ibid., 72–73; also Stronstad, *Baptized and Filled*, 35–36.

31. Stronstad, *Charismatic Theology*, 81.

Shelton also regards the Spirit's role in Luke's portrayal as including directing and enabling. The former concept is broad. It covers the overall direction of the church's mission and the specific directing of individuals in it. The enabling is to perform miracles, but is primarily for witness.[32] However, Shelton goes further than Stronstad in broadening his view of the Spirit's role to include not only what the Spirit accomplishes through recipients, but also what the Spirit gives to them. Thus the Spirit grants joy and enables celebratory prayer and praise.[33]

In conclusion, Stronstad's and Shelton's overall views of the Spirit's equipping are fairly broad in comparison to Menzies' (see below), and as such more accurate. This is reflected in Stronstad's preference for the term *charismatic* over *prophetic* (Menzies' favored term) and in Shelton's title: *Mighty in Word and Deed*. The Spirit, as portrayed by Luke, enables the performance of the church's mission and other tasks by initiating and directing every step, by equipping believers to preach boldly and perform miracles, and more generally by supplying whatever strengths, skills, or qualities may be necessitated by the tasks to which believers are called. The Spirit also grants to believers the subjective experience of joy and praise that accompanies their service.

Enabling in What Sense?—Menzies

Compared to Stronstad and Shelton, Menzies is less convincing, for his concepts of both the nature and purpose of the enabling are more narrow. The principal difference between his concept and that envisaged by Stronstad and Shelton is that in his view Luke did not portray the Spirit as directly associated with the performance of miracles. Menzies sees the gift of the Spirit, as conceptualized by Luke, in continuity with what he gleans from second temple Jewish literature, and that is best characterized by the label *Spirit of prophecy*. The gift granted knowledge by revelation from God and the ability to communicate it. However, as has already been observed, Luke and his readers may not have been as directly indebted to Jewish pneumatology as Menzies supposes. Turner

---

32. Shelton, *Mighty in Word and Deed*, 125–27.

33. Ibid., 125, 148, 157. He refers to Luke 10:21; Acts 11:23, 2; 13:52. Turner will agree with him.

suggests that Luke owed his view of the Spirit of prophecy to "hellenistic-Jewish Christian circles."[34] This is more plausible.[35]

Not only is Luke's immediate conceptual background more likely to be primitive Christian than non-Christian Jewish, but Menzies' exegesis of Luke's words concerning Spirit, power, and miracles is less than convincing. Menzies follows Schweizer in declaring that "Luke nowhere attributes exorcisms or miracles of healings to the work of the Spirit."[36] This is understandable, in view of Luke's repeated references to "power" as the source of miraculous healings (e.g., Luke 5:17; 6:19; 8:46; etc.). Also, not surprisingly, Menzies sees Luke's use of Mark 3:29 (where the context is exorcism) at Luke 12:10 (where the context is speech) and the wording of Luke 11:20 ("finger of God") in comparison with Matthew 12:28 ("Spirit of God") as strong supporting evidence.[37] For Luke, it was God's *power* rather than the *Spirit* to which miracles were attributed. When Luke used the terms *Spirit* and *power* together, as at Acts 10:38, they were not synonymous. The Spirit enabled prophecy, while the power enabled miracles.[38] "Luke takes great care not to associate the Spirit directly with the broader dimensions of the miraculous."[39]

However, this reconstruction does not do justice to the following passages.

34. Turner, "Spirit and the Power of Authoritative Preaching," 87. While Menzies understands Luke's emphasis on the Spirit as the power behind authoritative preaching to be completely in line with the Jewish concept of the Spirit of prophecy (Menzies, *Development*, 169), Turner has published important evidence suggesting otherwise: the typically Jewish view was that the Spirit was the organ of communication from God to a human and sometimes empowered "invasive" prophecy and praise, but did not directly enable preaching of a more considered nature (Turner, "Spirit and the Power of Authoritative Preaching," 76–87).

35. Ironically, Turner offers indications (Turner, "Spirit and the Power of Jesus' Miracles," 132–35) that Menzies may have misread the Jewish concept of the Spirit of prophecy, at this point anyway, because "for a Jew to hold that the Spirit was received as the Spirit of prophecy did not preclude him from attributing miracles to the same Spirit" (Turner, "Spirit and the Power of Jesus' Miracles," 135, with reference to Judg 14:6 LXX; Gen 1:2 LXX, etc.).

36. Menzies, *Development*, 124; Menzies, *Empowered for Witness*, 112. Compare Schweizer, *Holy Spirit*, 59.

37. Menzies, *Development*, 124, 185–98; Menzies, *Empowered for Witness*, 112, 161–63.

38. Menzies, *Development*, 125; Menzies, *Empowered for Witness*, 113.

39. Ibid., 113.

a. Luke 1:17. Luke attributed power but no miracles to John the Baptist.

b. Luke 1:35. In seeking to distance the Spirit from the miraculous conception, Menzies is forced to portray the Spirit as the source not so much of Mary's pregnancy as of her prophecy (Luke 1:46–55).[40] This is strained.

c. Luke 4:14. This and other verses (e.g., Acts 1:8) force Menzies to concede that "for Luke, the Holy Spirit is the source of 'power.'"[41] If this is so, "It is no longer easy to see how his [Menzies'] affirmation that the Spirit is the Spirit of prophecy and the source of *dunamis* ['power'] (which in turn is the source of miracles) differs meaningfully from the simpler affirmation that 'Luke regards the Spirit as both the Spirit of prophecy and the power of miracles.'"[42]

d. Luke 4:18. While Menzies rightly criticizes Turner for failing to provide an adequate reason for the omission of *iasasthai tous suntetrimmenous tēn kardian* ("to heal the crushed in heart") from the quotation of Isaiah 61:1, LXX,[43] this does not make Menzies' reason—that a reference to miracle is thus eliminated—correct. Clearly, as Turner points out, *iasasthai* ("to heal") in the context of broken hearts is metaphorical, however Luke may normally have used *iaomai* ("heal").[44] Furthermore, *apostelle tethrausmenous en aphesei* ("to send the oppressed into release"; Isa 58:6, LXX) probably includes miracles. If, as Menzies suggests, the liberation is limited to forgiveness,[45] Luke would have written *aphesei hamartiōn* ("release from sins").

---

40. Menzies, *Development*, 127–28; Menzies, *Empowered for Witness*, 115–16. Cf. Turner, "Spirit and the Power of Jesus' Miracles," 142 n. 44.

41. Menzies, *Development*, 125; Menzies, *Empowered for Witness*, 114.

42. Turner, "Spirit and the Power of Jesus' Miracles," 140–41.

43. Menzies, *Development*, 171. Turner, "Luke and the Spirit," 70, writes that "the elimination . . . allows room for the addition . . . of the extract of Isa 58.6." In Turner, "Spirit and the Power of Jesus' Miracles," 147, Turner confesses ignorance.

44. Turner, "Luke and the Spirit," 60; Turner, "Spirit and the Power of Jesus' Miracles," 173.

45. Menzies, *Development*, 173.

e. Acts 1:8. Here, Luke implied that *dunamis* ("power") was the ability to speak. If power was so closely linked in Luke's mind with *pneuma* ("Spirit") that the activities of the latter could be ascribed to the former, it seems implausible that Luke would not have been prepared to ascribe miracles directly to *pneuma* as well.

f. Acts 8:39. Here, the Spirit physically moved Philip from one place to another. Menzies is forced to appeal to the Western text: *pneuma hagion epepesen epi ton eunouchon, angelos de kuriou hērpasen ton Philippon* ("[the] Holy Spirit fell upon the eunuch, and an angel of the Lord carried Philip off").[46] However, the Western text of Acts is clearly weaker than the Alexandrian one in numerous ways, and thus less trustworthy.[47]

g. Acts 13:9–11. Here, the Spirit is most naturally understood as the source of the miracle, as well as of Paul's words.[48]

In conclusion, Menzies' understanding of the Spirit's enablement is too narrow. The gift of the Spirit was indeed a prophetic endowment, guiding the church by speaking to and through its members, and enabling effective preaching. However, this did not exclude the idea that the Spirit also enabled all of the church's miraculous deeds.[49]

Menzies' view of the purpose for which the Spirit was given is also strictly limited: it was that all recipients might "participate effectively in the missionary enterprise of the church."[50] This is undoubtedly correct in what it affirms. It reflects accurately not only the programmatic import of Acts 1:8, but also the whole thrust of the later narrative. However, Menzies' repetitive insistence that this is *the* purpose for which the Spirit was given[51] is incorrect in what it implicitly denies. There is evidence

46. Menzies, *Development*, 124; cf. Menzies, *Empowered for Witness*, 113.

47. See, e.g., Witherington, *Acts*, 65–68.

48. Menzies is wise to be tentative ("it can also be argued") in distinguishing the hand of the Lord from the Spirit, so that the "action of the Spirit on Paul . . . has an exclusively prophetic sense" (Menzies, *Empowered for Witness*, 112–13).

49. A similar assessment of Menzies' position is offered by Stronstad (Stronstad, *Prophethood of All Believers*, 61 n. 6).

50. Menzies, *Development*, 279; Menzies, *Empowered for Witness*, 227. By this "enterprise" Menzies clearly means the church's evangelistic mission to the unsaved. See, e.g., *Development*, 226 n. 5, 259–60.

51. Menzies, *Development*, 244, 245, 248, 260, 263, 267, etc.; *Empowered for Witness*, 201, 212, 218, 224, etc.

that Luke also thought of the Spirit as the church's guide in the conduct of its own affairs (e.g., Acts 6:3, 5; 11:28; 15:28). Some of this evidence receives little attention from Menzies, who is otherwise thorough.[52]

Furthermore, while Menzies is right to conclude that Luke presented the Spirit as received "principally for the benefit of others,"[53] his argumentation up to that point suggests that by "principally" he means "solely." Luke offered a greater place to the ministry of the Spirit to recipients, as opposed to through them, than Menzies admits. This departure is apparent in a number of passages. Two Lukan summaries suggest the Spirit's ministry towards the recipients themselves: Acts 9:31; 13:52. While Menzies may be right, from Acts 9:31, to attribute the church's growth to the Spirit's *paraklēsis* ("encouragement"; although from the evidence of this verse the growth was as much attributable to the church's fear of the Lord),[54] he is surely speculating when he attributes the expansion of Acts 13:49 to the joyful reception of the Spirit recorded in Acts 13:52.[55] Menzies also rather distorts Luke's picture of the Samaritan and Ephesian episodes. For Menzies, Acts 8:14–17 and 19:1–6 record not so much the urgent apostolic correction of anomalous defects in Christian initiation as ceremonies commissioning missionaries.[56] His evidence is not impressive. Both episodes involved the laying on of hands. In Acts, he claims, this event directly signified only healing or commissioning. As healing was clearly irrelevant to Acts 8:17 and 19:6, missionary commissioning must have applied in these two cases.[57] But Menzies offers no firm argument that Luke did not associate laying on of hands with the reception of the Spirit as such.[58] Further evidence that Menzies offers is

52. Acts 15:28 is mentioned in *Development*, in a list, in just one footnote, where also Acts 5:3, 9 gain their only individual attention. Menzies admits that in Acts 5:3, 9 "the Spirit undoubtedly influences the religious and ethical life of the Christian community" (Menzies, *Development*, 224 n. 2; Menzies, *Empowered for Witness*, 258). In Menzies, *Empowered for Witness*, Menzies includes Acts 15:28 in a list at 188 n. 2 that causes him to note, "Guidance is often attributed directly to the Spirit."

53. Menzies, *Development*, 279; Menzies, *Empowered for Witness*, 227. See especially Acts 1:8; 4:8, 31; 5:32; 6:3, 10; 11:24, 28; 13:9; 20:28; 21:4, 11.

54. Menzies, *Development*, 226 n. 5, 260 n. 2; Menzies, *Empowered for Witness*, 187 n. 4, 213 n. 1.

55. Menzies, *Development*, 225 n. 2, continued from 224.

56. Ibid., 259; Menzies, *Empowered for Witness*, 212, 224.

57. Menzies, *Development*, 259; *Empowered for Witness*, 212.

58. Menzies' reasoning (Menzies, *Development*, 259; Menzies, *Empowered for Witness*, 212) that, while healing (e.g., Acts 28:8) and commissioning (e.g., Acts 6:6) may

frail. Acts 9:31 includes Samaria in a summary statement about the growing church. For Menzies, this confirms his conclusion,[59] but Luke used no device of narrative composition to attach this statement specifically to Acts 8:4–25, or indeed to any other particular episode. The Ephesian converts formed, for Menzies, the core of the group who accompanied Paul from the synagogue (Acts 19:9) and of the elders who wept at Paul's departure (Acts 20:37). This may be true, but Menzies is wrong to claim that Luke highlighted these facts.[60] What Luke highlighted was not the missionary activities of the Ephesian converts, but their immediate religious experience, as displayed vocally (Acts 19:6; compare 10:46). One can safely surmise their missionary activity from Acts 1:8, but not from more immediate texts.

In summary, Menzies is right to state that the Spirit is granted to aid the missionary expansion of the church and as such is an anointing for the benefit of those as yet untouched. However, this correct emphasis must not overshadow Luke's other concerns: the Spirit brings joy, comfort, and worship to recipients and guides them in their concern for one another as well as for the wider world. Menzies' contribution is to be valued for what it emphasizes, but needs to be treated with caution regarding what it excludes.

TURNER'S "SOTERIOLOGICAL SPIRIT"

Turner's 1996 position is that, while there is an emphasis in Luke's mind on mission, this must not be allowed to color unduly our understanding of his "soteriological" pneumatology, for two reasons: first, only certain believers are portrayed as actively involved in the evangelistic mission of the church. Secondly, Luke links Spirit reception very firmly with Christian initiation, and this is simply incomprehensible if the gift of the Spirit is "merely" for the work of evangelism. There must, claims Turner, be a further explanation. In 1980, it is not offered, but by 1996, Turner

---

each be integral to laying on of hands, Spirit reception cannot be, because the Spirit is sometimes granted without the rite (e.g., Acts 10:44) and the rite does not always confer the Spirit (e.g., Acts 6:6), is inconsistent. Healing may also be conferred without the rite (e.g., Acts 5:15; 9:40), while clearly the rite does not always confer healing (e.g., Acts 6:6; 8:17; 19:6). Thus healing is no more integral to the laying on of hands than is Spirit reception. See also, briefly, Turner, "Prayer in the Gospels and Acts," 72.

59. Menzies, *Development*, 260; Menzies, *Empowered for Witness*, 213.

60. Ibid., 225.

has articulated this alternative. It is that, as believers have no direct access to Jesus after the ascension except by the Spirit,[61] such access must in effect be the Spirit's primary ministry to believers: no Christian in Acts could relate to Jesus other than by the gift of the Spirit. This gift must therefore in effect be soteriologically necessary. Turner is not here agreeing with Dunn in theory, but the practical outworking of his view brings him remarkably close to Dunn, so that in 2010 he can comment that he essentially agrees with Dunn.[62]

What are we to make of Turner's claims? In the previous chapter I tackled Turner's first claim, that the incongruity between all believers receiving the Spirit and only a few being actively involved in evangelism suggests "power-for-mission" cannot be regarded as the primary purpose of Spirit reception for Luke.[63] Turner's second claim, that Jesus could only be experienced after the ascension by the gift of the Spirit, thus making this gift soteriologically necessary, requires a much fuller response, and much of the rest of this chapter will be given over to this task.

First, a methodological point: Turner actually provides some of the armory that can be used in resisting his argument. He points out that for Luke "receiving the Spirit" was not a statement about the joining of two persons, on a par for instance with marriage. It was a functional metaphor: a metaphor of the inception of a new nexus of activities by the Spirit in the person who is described as "receiving the Spirit."[64] This observation by Turner is most helpful. It immediately opens up the possibility that Luke, or any user of the term, might acknowledge that the Spirit has *already* been performing other works in that person, or has perhaps been performing *some* of the associated works whose whole nexus will justify the term "receiving" without operating them *all*, before that occasion when the *complete* nexus of activities first occurs and the

61. Turner justifiably discounts the possibility that "the name" of Jesus could serve as the experiential link between the ascended Christ and earthly believers (Turner, *Power from on High*, 423–27).

62. "Dunn is right: it all comes down to the Spirit. I would qualify: The Spirit as the Spirit of prophecy is essentially the giver of all charismatic revelation, wisdom, and inspired speech. But he is fundamentally right: it is the Spirit, in Luke, who brings us into our experience of the 'kingdom of God'. For Luke, the Spirit is not just a *superadditum* for mission" (Turner, "James Dunn's *Baptism*," 31).

63. My counter-argument was that more were involved in evangelism, even if only at the level of "teamwork," than Turner allows.

64. Turner, "Luke and the Spirit," 35–40.

person can validly be said to have received the Spirit. It is thus important to consider what works of the Spirit Luke might have been implying occurred in a person before that whole nexus of activities operated that he termed "receiving the Spirit."

Luke reserved Spirit reception language for what he described primarily as a permanent[65] empowering. However, he did sometimes implicitly indicate that the Spirit was directly[66] at work in someone *prior* to what he called that person's reception of the Spirit.[67] This observation is a key one in considering the soteriological necessity of receiving the Spirit, and so I will now give some time to exploring what I consider to be "prior works" of the Spirit in people's lives—in other words, works that Luke would naturally attribute to the Spirit occurring in people before they had, in Luke's words, "received," been "baptized with," or been "filled with" the Spirit. I want to stress that I am not arguing here that Luke knew of two Spirit receptions in the lives of converts: a silent one at the inception of their new faith and an evidenced one as a potentially subsequent empowering for mission. Turner points out, accurately,[68] that Luke never wrote of two distinct initial Spirit receptions for believers.[69] I am

65. Luke implies that, excepting Elizabeth (Luke 1:41) and Zechariah (Luke 1:67), both Christ's predecessors (John [Luke 1:15]; Simeon [Luke 2:25]), Jesus himself (Luke 3:22; 4:1, 14, 18), and all of Jesus' followers received the Spirit permanently. Only one of Jesus' disciples had his fullness of the Spirit traced right through to his death: Stephen (Acts 6:5, 10; 7:55). Nevertheless, the permanent influence of the Spirit in Christians may be inferred from the text of Acts, in which activities characteristic of the Spirit's presence occurred amongst these Christians in the long term.

66. Of course, any person who heard the preaching of a Spirit-filled believer was thus being influenced by the Spirit *indirectly*. See Turner, *Power from on High*, 333–41. Turner claims that such a mediated influence of the Spirit might be as powerful as the immediate. This is debatable.

67. The argument that, if the Spirit was directly active in someone, that person must have thereby or already received the Spirit fails to recognize the sense with which Luke employed the metaphor. Spirit reception was "the *inception* of a . . . coherent set of activities of the Spirit" (Turner, *Power from on High*, 47; italics his). The metaphor does not thereby imply the complete absence of any one of those activities beforehand.

68. Turner, *Holy Spirit and Spiritual Gifts*, 152–57, 161–62.

69. Luke referred to only one individual receiving the Spirit in two distinct ways. This was Jesus, who received the Spirit as a preparation for his public ministry (Luke 3:22; 4:18), and, after his exaltation, received the Spirit to pour out on others (Acts 2:33). This was of course a unique case, as presented by Luke, for Jesus had thus become Lord of the Spirit, and the Spirit could now be termed the "Spirit of Jesus" (Acts 16:7). Luke did write of Christians receiving the Spirit more than once (e.g., Peter three times [Acts 2:4; 4:8, 31]; Paul twice [Acts 9:17; 13:9]), but these were not in distinctly different ways,

forwarding a subtly different thesis: that Luke recognized and wrote of direct activities in people's lives, prior to their reception of the Spirit, that he would understand as the Spirit's work. Having surveyed a number of relevant passages, I will then relate my findings to Turner's assertion that the gift of the Spirit in Acts was soteriologically necessary.

The Spirit at Work in Jesus

The first such implication can be seen in the life of Jesus. Luke recorded no reception of the Spirit by Jesus until after he was baptized by John (Luke 3:22). It is, of course, true that Luke presented him as conceived by the Spirit, but it must be borne in mind that Luke declared this to be the result of an action of the Holy Spirit upon *Mary*, not upon Jesus himself (Luke 1:35). Also, although Jesus was already called "Christ" before the Jordan anointing (Luke 2:11, 26), this must be understood as a proleptic title rather than as a statement of action already achieved (on the same basis, "there was born to you today a Savior who is Christ the Lord" [Luke 2:11] is not to be understood as conveying the idea that Jesus had already worked salvation). It is thus not true to Luke's narration to state, as Turner does,[70] that Jesus first "received" the Holy Spirit from his mother's womb. However, was the Spirit at work in Jesus' life prior to his Jordan experience?

The first two chapters of Luke's Gospel were crafted to indicate that Jesus was greater than John.[71] Given this deliberate portrayal of Jesus' superiority, we meet a surprise turn in two identically worded summary statements. Of John, Luke wrote: "and the child grew and became strong *pneumati* ['in S/spirit']" (Luke 1:80). Of Jesus, he only wrote: "and the

---

as is clear from each context. Neither did Luke imply that, for instance in the case of Peter, the Spirit departed after Acts 2:4 and then reappeared at Acts 4:8. Peter was clearly characteristically full of the Spirit (note the activities at Acts 2:14; 3:6, 12–26), and 4:8 simply indicates a particular invasive intensification of the Spirit's ongoing activity in Peter's life.

70. "Jesus had already received the Spirit in some fundamental way in Lk.1.35" (Turner, *Power from on High*, 434; cf. Turner, *Holy Spirit and Spiritual Gifts*, 154).

71. Elizabeth was barren (Luke 1:7); Mary was a virgin (Luke 1:34). John was "great in the sight of the Lord" (Luke 1:15); Jesus was "great and . . . called the Son" (Luke 1:32). John was filled with the Spirit from his mother's womb (Luke 1:15); Jesus was conceived by the Spirit (Luke 1:35). John was a "prophet of the Most High" (Luke 1:32); Jesus was "the Son of the Most High" (Luke 1:76). John was to be a granter of the knowledge of salvation (Luke 1:77); Jesus was to be God's salvation (Luke 2:30). See Fitzmyer, *Gospel according to Luke I–IX*, 313–14.

child grew and became strong, being filled with wisdom" (Luke 2:40). We might at least expect Luke here to have told us that Jesus, too, was growing in the Spirit. Luke was avoiding *pneuma* ("S/spirit") terminology in the case of Jesus, but not in the case of John. This might have been because John had already received the Spirit (Luke 1:15), and Jesus had not. However, Luke was not avoiding mention of a divine activity (filling with wisdom) that he was happy on other occasions to attribute to the Spirit (e.g., Acts 6:3;[72] 15:28). The same terminological caution but conceptual freedom is seen at Luke 2:52, where Jesus was said to grow "in wisdom."[73]

In one other case prior to his reception of the Spirit was Jesus the object of divine activity that elsewhere Luke attributed to the Spirit. At the age of twelve, Jesus entered into debate with the teachers in the temple. Two points are relevant. Everyone was "amazed at his understanding and his answers" (Luke 2:47). This was further evidence of the wisdom that we might elsewhere expect Luke to associate explicitly with the work of the Spirit. And when challenged by his mother, who called Joseph his father (Luke 2:48), Jesus displayed awareness that God was his father (Luke 2:49). It is not so clear that Luke openly related knowledge of God's fatherhood to the work of the Spirit,[74] but if the dove from heaven was the herald of the voice from above that said "You are my son" (Luke

72. "Full of the Spirit and wisdom" could be taken to mean that these were two independent "commodities" granted separately and merely coincidentally to Stephen by God. However, the phrase "Spirit and wisdom" can more reasonably be understood as a hendiadys, giving the overall sense of "full of wisdom by the Spirit" (so Turner, *Power from on High*, 408 n. 21). This is in keeping with the traditional Jewish concept of the Spirit of prophecy, which, once further hellenized and christianized, most probably formed the basis on which Luke's pneumatology rested (see Turner, *Power from on High*, ch. 3).

73. It is tempting to speculate about Luke's reasons for avoiding such language at these points. Turner, noting the presumed work of the Spirit in Christ's giving his disciples power and authority (Luke 9:1), offers the straightforward suggestion that Luke was avoiding confusion with his narration of the later gift at Pentecost (Turner, *Power from on High*, 336). By analogy, Luke might here be avoiding confusion with his account of the Jordan anointing.

74. That such a work of the Spirit might be part of the traditional understanding of the Spirit of prophecy is hinted in *T. Levi* 18:6–7 ("The heavens will be opened, and from the temple of glory sanctification will come upon him, with a fatherly voice, as from Abraham to Isaac. And the glory of the Most High shall burst forth upon him. And the spirit of understanding and sanctification shall rest upon him"); *T. Jud.* 24:2 ("And the heavens will be opened upon him to pour out the spirit as a blessing of the Holy Father"). Translations from Charlesworth, *Pseudepigrapha Vol. I*, 795, 801.

3:22), then he did. He may also have indicated this in Luke 10:21–22, where Luke's redaction juxtaposed fullness of the Spirit with awareness of God's fatherhood (cf. Matt 11:25).

In conclusion to this section, Luke did not present Jesus as receiving the Spirit until just after his baptism. Nevertheless, before this event, Jesus was shown to be the object of divine activities that Luke elsewhere attributed to the Spirit. Luke avoided the term *pneuma* ("S/spirit") in these descriptions,[75] but was not unwilling to present, by way of other terms, the *concept* of the Spirit's activity. Luke seemed to be hinting, with careful caution, that the Spirit was active in Jesus before the inception of the outstanding nexus of activities that Luke would label as the actual arrival of the Spirit in Jesus' life.

The Spirit at Work in the Disciples

One can detect a similar cautious hint of the Spirit's work in the lives of the disciples prior to their Pentecostal reception. When sending the Twelve out to preach the kingdom and heal the sick, Jesus gave them "power and authority over all the demons and to heal diseases" (Luke 9:1). This may seem unrelated to the work of the Spirit in two ways: it was Jesus, not the Spirit, who gave the power, and what was given was power *for the miraculous*, which, as I noted earlier in the chapter, Menzies sees as distanced by Luke from the work of the Spirit.

The latter consideration—that Luke here mentioned power as the gift rather than the Spirit—must not lead us to consider that he wrote of a significantly different concept. Luke was willing to link *pneuma* ("S/spirit") with *dunamis* ("power") in a variety of ways, from Luke 1:17 onwards. Even before the Twelve were sent out, Jesus' power to cast out demons (Luke 4:36) had been presented by Luke as the work of the Spirit: the Spirit granted Jesus power, and that power, among other things, enabled him to "release the oppressed" (Luke 4:14, 18). Also, his power to raise the dead was interpreted by the Lukan crowds as evidence that a prophet was among them (Luke 7:14–16; cf. 24:19), and prophecy,

75. Discussion about whether Luke was faithfully reproducing wording from his source(s) or was creating his own wording at this point is not useful, because the sources Luke used in compiling the infancy narratives are unavailable for study. Also, redaction criticism indicates, where Luke's sources are available for comparison, that Luke was ready to alter wording to suit his purposes if he so wished. Thus where he left traditional wording alone that was a choice that must be taken as an indicator of Luke's preferred way of presenting his material.

of all activities, lay at the heart of the Lukan teaching on the functions of the outpoured Spirit (note, above all, the repetition of "and they will prophesy" in Acts 2:18: see ch. 2). Later, Jesus offered a promise of further power to the disciples (Luke 24:49) that was likely to remind them of the power they received for their earlier ventures.[76] Yet this promise of power was clearly interpreted in terms of the Spirit's future arrival (Acts 1:4–8).[77]

It is now necessary to tackle the question about whether Luke 9:1 has any relevance to the work of the Spirit, when it was explicitly *Jesus* who granted the power and authority to the disciples on this occasion.

76. Stronstad also points out that this promised power would reflect the power which Jesus himself ministered in, a power which itself had been conveyed to him by the Spirit (Stronstad, *Prophethood of All Believers*, 37–38). One must be cautious here, for both uses of the word "power" at Luke 4:14 and Luke 9:1 are the narrator's (probably Lukan), not the characters'. Luke may not have regarded *power* as a word Jesus or his disciples would have used at the time of these experiences (though note Luke 8:46; 10:13).

77. One wonders what, in the apostles' subjective experience (as understood by Luke), was the difference between receiving power (Luke 9:1) and receiving the Spirit (Acts 2:4). In other words, what was missing from the earlier experience so that it was not, to use Turner's terminology, the whole nexus of pneumatic activities that would warrant use of the phrase, "receive the Holy Spirit"? Clearly, they did not on that first occasion lack the ability to preach or heal (Luke 9:1–2). One assumes they had sufficient boldness, and that the difference was not that they preached timidly in Luke 9 and boldly in Acts 2. One can only assume, with Turner, that the difference was the sense of the presence of Jesus. In Luke 9, they knew full well that while they were in village A, Jesus was in village B; and there were no modern means of communication to link them! They had the assurance that Jesus had commissioned them only days before, and they had what might have been for them an amazing, exciting, and possibly puzzling ability to do what they had only those few days before been watching Jesus do, but what they *lacked* was any sense that Jesus was right there with them. They could, of course, talk together about his teaching. They could remember individually and corporately his acts of power, but that was all. In Acts, after Pentecost, we are led by Luke to believe that they actually felt Jesus in their midst and "in their hearts." This realization leads us to acknowledge a considerably broader view of the post-Pentecost Spirit's role than, say, Menzies admits. However, it is by no means necessary to go with Turner at this point and say that the reception of this gift is "soteriologically necessary." Luke hints that one could come to faith in who Jesus was (such as this was understood at this very early stage in the life of the church) and what he had done (most particularly this meant believing that he had risen from the dead and ascended to the Father) without having an inner sense of the presence of this man in one's life. For that, we assume, one needed to receive the Spirit, who would "also" grant extraordinary ability to witness boldly and go beyond one's natural limitations in Christian service. For those apostles, it was not merely "Luke 9 all over again." It was a quality of life that would have been impossible, in its full expression, while Jesus walked the hills and valleys of Galilee.

It is important to consider how Luke might have conceived of Jesus giving this power, especially as it was a power that the disciples were to operate at a geographical distance from Jesus himself, once on the village-to-village mission. It was not a quasi-physical commodity that he could leave in their laps. Luke might mean simply that Jesus prayed authoritatively for them to receive power, but his language does not seem to convey such an idea. It appears more likely that Luke thought of Jesus giving this power by means of the very Spirit with whom he was himself anointed.[78] Jesus was passing on something of the power and authority that he, by the Spirit, had up to then been exercising. If this is the case, Luke was hinting at an operation of the Spirit in the lives of the disciples prior to their Pentecostal reception of the Spirit.[79]

At Luke 24:45 a similar impression is formed. The text again declares that it was Jesus who opened the disciples' minds, rather than the Spirit. A physical act, though, is clearly not in view! Luke was later to suggest that Jesus was instructing his disciples through the Spirit (Acts 1:2). It is reasonable to suppose, therefore, that this opening of their minds—a direct influence in them—also occurred by agency of the Spirit. Elsewhere, Luke presented the opening of the mind to understand the word and will of God wisely as an unequivocal work of the Spirit (Acts 6:3; 15:28; 20:23; 21:11).

As with Jesus, then, so with the disciples: Luke carefully avoided the term *pneuma* ("Spirit") in describing these divine activities in the lives of Christ's pre-Pentecost followers. But he did not avoid the concept of the Spirit's typical operations. Rather, he offered broad hints that the Spirit could be at work in a life prior to the promised reception of the Spirit in that life.

78. Turner's agreement with this point has been noted in ch. 2. In some contrast, Fitzmyer suggests that, "his commission gives them a share in his 'power' and 'authority'" (Fitzmyer, *Gospel according to Luke I–IX*, 752). It is difficult to see how the commission as such could convey the power.

79. Jeremias sees sayings in the Gospels which "presuppose that the possession of the spirit has been communicated to the disciples" (Jeremias, *New Testament Theology*, Vol. 1, 79). Amongst these he includes Luke 6:23, 26, "which put the disciples in the ranks of the prophets." Jeremias sees "the bestowing of the spirit on the disciples during the lifetime of Jesus" as an early tradition, in conflict with the tradition that the Spirit was given at Pentecost (ibid., 80). Whatever the provenance of the tradition, Luke retained it, though, of course, redacted to avoid *pneuma* ("Spirit") terminology, as noted.

The Spirit at Work in Later Lives

Luke provided similar hints in his narration of the mission of the church after Pentecost. A particularly strong hint concerning the Spirit's prior work comes at Acts 9:10–19. Ananias, a disciple and therefore presumably in receipt of the Spirit, had a vision in which he heard the Lord calling. That Ananias should have a vision was in perfect accord with the explanation, given by Peter on the day of Pentecost with reference to Joel 2:28–32, that the arrival of the Spirit ushered in a plethora of prophetic activity including seeing visions (Acts 2:17). It is perhaps, then, a little more surprising to find Paul, at Acts 9:12, also having a vision. Paul was only to receive the Spirit once Ananias had reached him (Acts 9:17). Yet prior to his Spirit reception Paul was already the object of divine activity for which Luke elsewhere offered only one explanation: visions come by the Holy Spirit (Acts 2:17).[80] Acts 26:16–18 is consistent with this, for here Luke presented the voice of Jesus giving many clear directive words to Paul while he was still lying on the Damascus road. Elsewhere in Luke's works, this prophetic infusion was characteristically given by agency of the Spirit (Acts 20:23; 21:11, etc.).

Cornelius too had a vision before he received the Spirit.[81] When Luke presented Cornelius' narration of this apparition, the words used were "a man in bright clothes" (Acts 10:30). Angelic visitations, according to Luke, could occur quite apart from the agency of the Spirit (Luke 1:11, 26–27; Acts 1:10). However, when Luke himself acted as narrator of Cornelius' experience, he chose to write of a "vision" of an angel (Acts 10:3), a term that, as I showed above, the reader, prompted by Luke, associates naturally with the work of the Spirit.

There are one or two references in Acts to the conversion of people whose reception of the Spirit was not narrated, but in whose lives a work of the Spirit may be glimpsed before their presumed reception. Lydia is a prime example: "Lydia . . . a worshipper of God was listening. The Lord opened her heart to pay attention to what Paul was saying. When she and her household were baptized, she pleaded, 'If you have judged me to

80. Admittedly, Acts 2:17 uses *horasis* ("vision"), governed as it is by the wording of Joel 2:28 LXX. Acts 9:12 uses the similar word *horama* ("vision"; there is some textual doubt at this point).

81. Again the word used is *horama*. Turner actually denies that Cornelius' vision here was an activity of the Spirit, but his own advice to "avoid . . . multiplying hypotheses where one is sufficient" (Turner, "Luke and the Spirit," 138) applies here.

be a believer in the Lord, come and stay at my house'" (Acts 16:14–15). This divine opening of Lydia's heart could not refer to her actual reception of the Spirit, as this opening was the cause of her belief rather than a consequence and evidence of it, as Spirit reception would be (cf. Acts 15:8–9, as ably exegeted by Menzies[82]). But was it a work of the Spirit? It was narrated as a work of Jesus. The verbal coincidence between "the Lord opened her heart" (Acts 16:14) and "he opened their minds" (Luke 24:45) is noteworthy. Beyond the verbal coincidence, the immediate context indicates that "the Lord" refers to Jesus, not the Father or undifferentiated God.[83] This is evident from verse 14, which does not read, "a worshipper of God, who opened her heart." It also emerges from the words, "If you have judged me a believer in the Lord" in verse 15. Here, "Lord" clearly refers to Jesus, for Lydia was already a worshipper of God, and so Paul's verdict was demanded of her attitude to Jesus specifically.

That this opening of Lydia's heart can be viewed as a work of the Spirit may be argued both from its similarity to the wisdom-granting work of the Spirit already noted in connection with Christ's opening of the disciples' minds after the resurrection and also from the realization that the only way Jesus was explicitly presented in Acts as working on earth after his exaltation was by his Spirit.[84] As noted, Luke did not report Lydia's subsequent reception of the Spirit, but as Lydia was baptized (Acts 16:15), the reader is led to assume that she did indeed receive the gift, not least on the basis of the programmatic promise at Acts 2:38–39.[85]

---

82. See discussion in ch. 2. In short, Dunn states that "God's giving of the Holy Spirit is equivalent to his cleansing of their hearts" (Dunn, *Baptism*, 81–82); Menzies counters that "Verse 8 is the premise from which the deduction of v. 9 is drawn" (Menzies, *Empowered for Witness*, 217).

83. Against Turner, *Power from on High*, 410 n. 26. Of the 108 times the singular *kurios* ("Lord") is used in Acts, it is clear from the context that it refers to God the Father eight times (Acts 2:25 etc.), four of them in Old Testament contexts, and that it refers to Jesus forty-three times (Acts 1:6 etc.), seventeen times in the term *Lord Jesus*. On fifty-five occasions, it is debatable whether the context allows us to be firm about whether the referent is the Father or Jesus. Once, the term is used of an angel (Acts 10:4). The plural *kurioi* ("Sirs") can be used of people (e.g., Acts 16:30).

84. Especially at Acts 16:7. That Jesus spoke to Paul on the Damascus road by his Spirit has been argued above.

85. See discussion earlier in this chapter about reading conversions later in Acts in the light of 2:38.

A further example where the Spirit's work may be discernible prior to reception is at Acts 2:37: the people who heard Peter preach on the day of Pentecost were presented as having been "cut to the heart." Here too one might be justified in seeing the work of the Spirit in taking the message and using it to cut to the heart. A similar hint is to be found in the traditional view of the role of the Spirit of prophecy, on which, indirectly, Luke probably built.[86] This subsection, then, shows the same trait in Acts as found in the Gospel. In subtle ways, that avoid reference by name to the Holy Spirit, Luke nevertheless recognized the Spirit's work in someone even before that person had received the Pentecostal gift.

Conclusion

A fairly consistent picture has emerged. Luke was unwilling to state by name that the Holy Spirit was at work in the lives of those who, by his own description, had not yet received the Spirit. However, he was not unwilling to describe divine activities, which he generally attributed to the Holy Spirit elsewhere in his works, occurring in the lives of people at this stage. An important conclusion may be drawn from this observation, relating to Turner's position. The observations set out above undermine his conclusion that the reception of the Spirit (Turner's favorite term is the "gift of the Spirit," no doubt from Acts 2:38) is, in Luke's conception, soteriologically necessary.

Though throughout *Power from on High* Turner notes situations where the Spirit works prior to Spirit reception, his focus seems to be on cases where the Spirit's work in an individual or group is *indirect*.[87] He admits the possibility of the direct work of the Spirit in the pre-Pentecost disciples, but speculates that this activity is not worthy of the term *Spirit of Prophecy*, but must be limited to "God's liberating power at work through the disciples."[88] He overlooks the implied direct work of the Spirit of prophecy at, for example, Acts 9:12, even while attributing

---

86. "There is no moment in which man's works can be concealed, because they are written on the heart in the Lord's sight. And the spirit of truth testifies to all things and brings all accusations. He who has sinned is consumed in his heart and cannot raise his head to face the judge" (*T. Jud.* 20:4–5; translation from Charlesworth, *Pseudepigrapha*, Vol. I, 800).

87. See Turner, *Power from on High*, 417, 435; though cf. ibid., 423 and n. 56.

88. Ibid., 341.

Ananias' vision at Acts 9:10 to the Spirit,[89] and so when he discusses the soteriological necessity of the Spirit, he merely discusses the soteriological necessity of *receiving* the Spirit, without due recognition of any prior work. Turner accuses Pentecostals at this point of over-simplifying Luke,[90] but himself over-simplifies Luke, failing to note prior works that distance the reception of the Spirit, as conceptualized by Luke, from soteriological necessity. Turner implicitly sees the direct work of the Spirit of prophecy as absent prior to reception of the Pentecostal gift. Luke's frequent hints indicate otherwise. Turner is right to declare that Luke "thought the Spirit performed soteriological functions in the believer,"[91] but is wrong to tie these functions, in Luke's mind, to the moment of reception and beyond.

Turner would probably counter-argue that I, like other Pentecostals, am confusing the inception of salvation with salvation itself. He might concede that reception of the Pentecostal gift of the Spirit is not necessary for the inception of Christian faith, but would perhaps continue to assert that it is necessary for ongoing faith and active Christian life. However, while Pentecostals must not restrict their definitions of salvation too narrowly, neither must Turner "expand" his unduly. The accounts Luke offered both of Zacchaeus (Luke 19:9) and of the Philippian jailer (Acts 16:31) indicate, especially when taken together, that salvation could refer, in Luke's thinking, to an immediate change in relationship to Jesus and thereby to God. And we must not forget the Samaritans. While Luke may at times want to invest in the term *salvation* all the qualities of successful ongoing Christian life and experience (as Turner wants), Philip *baptized* the Samaritan converts—and Peter and John did not query this baptism, as far as we know. The implication is not that the Samaritans had yet received all they would need for successful ongoing Christian life and activity. However, it is that they *had* sufficiently engaged in the quality of life that Luke elsewhere calls salvation for mature Christians both to baptize them and recognize their baptism.[92]

89. Ibid., 423 n. 56.

90. Ibid., 433, 435.

91. Ibid., 438.

92. Turner's difficulty here is his overemphasis, following, for instance, the work of N. T. Wright, on corporate Jewish expectations of "salvation." These are undoubtedly testified to in Luke (e.g., 1:69–71; 2:25, 38), but whatever these pre-Christian Jewish expectations were, and however strong they were, they must not be allowed to drown out *Jesus'* concept of salvation, as expressed in Luke's writings.

In summary, Turner's 1996 alternative to Dunn's thesis is unsatisfactory in several respects. Most particularly, his claim that the Pentecostal gift of the Spirit, while not the immediate conveyor of new covenant life, is after all soteriologically necessary has turned out to be based on a reading of Luke that fails to take note of Luke's subtleties. With careful terminological caution, Luke's works indicate:

a. that the Spirit may be directly at work in the process of people's coming to faith;

b. that these new converts, despite such prior "soteriological" work of the Spirit, still need to *receive* the Pentecostal gift of the Spirit.

This is not a two-stage reception, but it is a two (or more) stage work.

CONCLUSIONS

Pentecostal alternatives to Dunn's thesis are not uniform. When the variations are studied, some varieties prove stronger than others. With respect to Christian initiation, Petts and Turner are more convincing than Stronstad. With respect to what exactly the empowering of the Spirit was for, Stronstad and Shelton are more accurate than, on the one hand, Menzies, for his concept is too narrow, and, on the other hand, Turner, whose concept somewhat misrepresents what Luke wrote, about both "prior works" of the Spirit and the inception of salvation.

The Pentecostal gift of the Spirit was linked programmatically to other aspects of Christian initiation (Acts 2:38, which must be allowed its full force). However, this did not mean that the early steps of discipleship could not occur without it (e.g., in Acts 8:4–24). However anomalous the Samaritan episode was, it indicates clearly both the conceptual distinctions to be drawn between coming to faith in Christ and receiving the Spirit, and the chronological gaps that this distinction then allows. This does not mean, for Luke, that the Spirit was inactive prior to someone's receiving the Spirit. The Spirit could perform individual acts, such as granting a vision or opening a heart, giving wisdom, or assuring of sonship (if Jesus' childhood experience may be extended by analogy to the experience of others), before the convert was filled with the Spirit in fulfillment of the Acts 1:8 promise. Thus the Spirit was, so to speak, soteriologically involved, but the Pentecostal reception of the Spirit was not soteriological. Ongoing Christian life, according to Luke's silence, was unknown without reception of the Spirit, but saving conversion could occur before this reception.

When the Spirit did arrive in this way—when the Pentecostal gift was granted—the recipients were enabled. They were enabled, programmatically, to take part in the worldwide evangelistic mission of the growing church (Acts 1:8). Clearly, this enabling included boldness in verbal witness (e.g., Acts 4:31), guidance in the conduct of the mission (e.g., Acts 16:6–10), and on occasion the ability to perform miracles of healing and exorcism (e.g., Acts 10:38, which by extension would apply to anointed disciples of Christ as well [Acts 1:1]) and even judgement (Acts 13:9–11). But the enabling was broader than that. As this chapter has shown, the Spirit also granted recipients joy, encouragement, and guidance in the internal affairs of the church. On the individual level, with Turner, the Spirit granted recipients their subjective awareness of the presence of Jesus, which no doubt played its part in emboldening them in their personal "mission" (see, for example, Acts 18:9–11, which, again by extension, might in Luke's eyes have been the experience of any Spirit-filled believer).

My examination of Dunn's debaters in this chapter has allowed a fairly clear picture of Luke's pneumatology to emerge. Now that this has happened, I can move on and consider in chapter 4 how Luke-Acts fits in its canonical context.

4

Luke-Acts in Its Canonical Context

INTRODUCTION

So far this book has been about Luke-Acts. We have seen that for Luke the phrase *receive the Spirit* was not a synonym for coming to faith in Christ. Nor was it the means by which God granted forgiveness to those who believed. Reception of the Spirit presupposed this faith, logically even if not always chronologically. The Spirit may have been at work in the process by which a person came to believe, but when Luke used the language of Spirit reception, he was referring to that nexus of activities that led the recipient into the fullness of Christian life and witness through charismatic empowerment to hear from God and to express this reality. While, ideally, this Spirit reception should be closely tied to the very beginnings of Christian life, Luke was aware that this was not always the case.

Such is Luke's contribution. But, of course, we Pentecostals, while admittedly operating in practice with something of a canon-within-the-canon,[1] wish to listen to the whole biblical canon in forming our pneumatology. Luke-Acts therefore has to be placed, so to speak, within its wider biblical context. The various voices of the Bible have to make room for one another. This is not to be compared to the polishing of pebbles on the beach, for each voice must be allowed to retain its possibly sharp distinctives, but it is to let the perspectives juxtapose in what will at times be a creative tension. My task in this chapter, then, is to relate Luke's perspective to those found elsewhere in the Christian Scriptures. However, for the sake of focus I will limit this task to the New Testament,

---

1. For discussion of Pentecostals' "canon-within-a-canon"—and those of other groups—see Mittelstadt, *Reading Luke-Acts*, 1–2 and n. 3.

and to only two other authors there: Paul and John. Nor will I study all that these two authors have to offer, but will take just one text from each of them as, in effect, a test case both for what that author's overall contribution may be, and for how that contribution may relate to that of Luke. In the case of Paul, I will consider 1 Corinthians 12:13; from the Fourth Gospel, John 20:22 will be my focus.

As in my previous chapters, I will look at these texts through the lens of James Dunn's writing on them in his *Baptism*, and of the Pentecostal responses to what he has written. One of the most striking aspects of the whole Pentecostal debate with Dunn is that, while Pentecostal exegetes have risen up almost in unison against his reading of Luke-Acts, the re-action to his exegesis of other New Testament passages has, with one or two exceptions, been much more muted. Some ignore (at least in print) what he writes of other authors. Some only go beyond Luke to interact with what Dunn writes of Paul. Ervin alone, of the Pentecostals under review here, considers all the New Testament references in Dunn's work. When response beyond Luke has occurred, it has often been to *agree* with Dunn. Pentecostals can disagree with Dunn regarding Luke and agree with him about Paul simply by seeing differences between Luke and Paul that Dunn is not prepared to acknowledge.

A TEST CASE: 1 CORINTHIANS 12:13

Dunn devotes a similar amount of space in *Baptism* to the writings of Paul as to those of Luke. He discusses every passage in the Pauline corpus that in his opinion alludes to conversion-initiation.[2] Again he believes he is on strong ground, asserting that for Pentecostal views of Spirit baptism, "Paul seems to be more of an embarrassment than an asset, so that time and again expositions of this doctrine conveniently ignore him."[3] For Dunn, when Paul's insights are duly noted, they "knock the Pentecostals' case on the head" and cut "the ground away from under the feet of the Pentecostal."[4] Perhaps the "killer blow" to Pentecostal doc-trine, in his view, is Romans 8:9. As he has written recently, "the nearest Paul comes to defining the term 'Christian' is in terms of having, that is,

2. While Dunn recognizes scholarly doubts about the authorship of Ephesians (Dunn, *Baptism*, 158) and the Pastoral letters (ibid., 167), he uses evidence from those letters to contribute to his overall picture of Paul (ibid., 170).

3. Ibid., 103.

4. Ibid., 123, 135.

of having received the Spirit: 'if anyone does not have the Spirit, he is not Christ's' (Rom. 8.9)."[5] However, while I will refer to Romans 8:9 later in this chapter, I will actually take 1 Corinthians 12:13 as my test case, for the simple reason that it is this text alone among Paul's writings that uses the phrase "baptized in [or 'with'] one Holy Spirit," and is therefore most likely to be understood by some Pentecostals as relating to "baptism in the Spirit."[6] Equally, however, it might be seen by other Pentecostals as, to quote Dunn, an embarrassment, or as a source of confusion or perplexity.

I will summarize Dunn's reading of this important text, and will then present the arguments of two Pentecostals—Ervin and Petts—who disagree with his exegesis. First, however, I will set out the key parts of the verse, in Greek and in an over-literal translation (I am presenting the verse so as to highlight the poetic quality that the Greek has. Even those who cannot read Greek will be able to see the similarity in the final words of the two Greek lines):

kai gar en heni pneumati hēmeis pantes eis hen sōma ebaptisthēmen . . .
kai pantes hen pneuma epotisthēmen

("For also in/with one Spirit we all into one body were baptized . . .
and all one Spirit given to drink.")

Dunn's Understanding of 1 Corinthians 12:13

In a lengthy section on this important text, Dunn describes and refutes Pentecostal interpretations that he has come across. Some take *en* (usually "in") in verse 13a to mean "by," so that this part of the verse is made to refer to conversion (a baptism performed *by* the Spirit), not baptism *in* the Spirit. This must probably be rejected, writes Dunn, for the use of *en* with *baptizō* ("baptize") in the New Testament generally points to the element *in* which people were immersed or *with* which they were deluged. Other Pentecostals accept that baptism in the Spirit is referred to, but unwarrantably translate *eis* (usually "into") in verse 13a as something other than "into," thereby removing initiatory connotations. Still others—and here Dunn specifically cites Ervin's 1968 *These Are Not Drunken, As Ye Suppose*—simply accept that Paul is not describing Pentecostal

---

5. Dunn, "Baptism Again," 36; cf. Dunn, *Romans 1–8*, 444.

6. As Dunn notes (Dunn, *Baptism*, 103).

baptism in the Spirit, but is referring to conversion. This is at least true to the text, states Dunn, but does no good for Pentecostalism, for in his view a distinction between Paul's use of the phrase and Luke's "undermines rather than supports that doctrine."[7] "In short, once the initiatory and incorporative significance of the metaphor is grasped, the Pentecostal arguments fall to the ground."[8] Dunn continues by discussing Paul's use of *potizō* (usually "give to drink"; "water") in verse 13c. This stands in parallel to the first part of the verse, and so it also refers to the Corinthians' experience of the Spirit in their conversion, which "was like the outpouring of a sudden flood or rainstorm on a parched ground."[9]

Ervin's Understanding of 1 Corinthians 12:13

This section refers partly to Ervin's view as presented in his 1984 response to Dunn, but also partly to Ervin's 1968 work, which, as I noted in the previous paragraph, Dunn had already interacted with in *Baptism*. Ervin regards the "poetic" parallelism in 1 Corinthians 12:13 as "synthetic" rather than "synonymous" (drawing on terms from the study of Hebrew poetic parallelism). In other words, the two verbs "were baptized" and "were given to drink" are not different expressions for the same experience but rather refer to different experiences. This he expresses clearly in *Not Drunken* (1968) and repeats virtually unaltered (and with no reference to Dunn) in *Spirit-Baptism* (1987). 1 Corinthians 12:13 "stresses two aspects of the Christian's relationship to the Holy Spirit. To be 'baptized in the Spirit' is to be placed in the sphere of the Holy Spirit, that is at conversion; while 'being given to drink of the Spirit' places the Spirit's fullness within the believer."[10] In responding to Dunn in *Conversion-Initiation*, Ervin accepts that verse 13a is correctly translated by Dunn and refers to conversion, although he wisely opposes Dunn concerning the relationship between Paul's and Luke's words: these two authors do not necessarily use the phrase to refer to the same experience.[11]

---

7. Dunn, *Baptism*, 129. Whether Dunn is right to assert that seeing a distinction between Lukan and Pauline language undermines Pentecostalism is moot. We will return to this matter later in the chapter.

8. Ibid., 129.

9. Ibid., 131.

10. Ervin, *These Are Not Drunken*, 46; Ervin, *Spirit-Baptism*, 32–33; similarly, Hunter, *Spirit Baptism*, 41–42 (59–60 in 2009 edn).

11. Ervin, *Conversion-Initiation*, 99, 101–2.

Ervin's main criticism of Dunn concerns verse 13c, and its use of *potizō* (usually "give to drink"; "water"). Ervin demurs.

a. To take this as a synonymous parallel of verse 13a is to create a "curious mixed-metaphor . . . of drinking one's way into the body."[12]

b. Dunn is wrong to translate *potizō* as to "pour" rather than to "drink." "If the meaning 'to pour out' is substituted for 'to drink,' the translation must then be, 'we (not the Spirit) were poured out.' Obviously this is *not* what the text is saying."[13]

Both of Ervin's criticisms are faulty. Concerning the first, the very nature of a metaphor is to juxtapose concepts that if taken "literally" would lead to absurdity. If drinking one's way into a body is absurd, so is being immersed (or deluged) into a body. Therefore the metaphors create no difficulty for seeing a "synonymous parallelism" in the verse, with both parts of the verse referring to the same experience.[14] Ervin's second criticism misrepresents Dunn (and not for the first time—see chapter 2). Dunn is not suggesting that verse 13c means, "we were poured out." Rather, Dunn is suggesting that it means "we had [the Spirit] poured out on us" or "we were watered [as in 'irrigated'] with the Spirit." Dunn regards this as a perfectly reasonable metaphor for people who were used to seeing rain refresh parched ground and bring new life, and who were familiar with the hopes expressed for instance in Isaiah 32:15.[15]

In conclusion, Ervin has not successfully undermined Dunn's work. The two passive verbs in 1 Corinthians 12:13 stand in straightforward poetic parallel with one another, as is suggested by the Greek word forms, and very probably refer to the same experience. In conceding to Dunn that verse 13a refers to initial incorporation, Ervin cannot con-

---

12. Ibid., 100; cf. Ervin, *Spirit-Baptism*, 32.

13. Ibid., 100.

14. So Fee, *First Epistle to the Corinthians*, 604–5; similarly Barrett, *Commentary on the First Epistle to the Corinthians*, 289. Fee notes that Ervin's view dates back at least to 1949 and the writing of Ralph Riggs (604 n. 26).

15. Dunn, *Baptism*, 131. Dunn's suggested translation here may be somewhat faulty, but not for the reasons Ervin offers. If the meaning was "we were all watered/irrigated with one Spirit," Paul would probably have written (*en*) *heni pneumati epotisthēmen*, which would have offered an even closer verbal parallel to verse 13a. Cf. Isa 29:10 LXX.

vincingly claim that verse 13c refers to a second work: a "Spirit baptism" as understood by Pentecostals.[16]

Petts' Understanding of 1 Corinthians 12:13

Petts follows a somewhat different line of reasoning. He disagrees with Dunn concerning verse 13a, and the translation of *en* (usually "in"). Grammatically, the preposition might be either locative (expressing whereabouts: "in") or instrumental (expressing means: "by"). The decision, Petts proposes, must be made on contextual grounds. The immediate context includes the instrumental use of *en* in 1 Corinthians 12:9 ("to another, faith [is given] *by* the same Spirit"). This contextual use supports an instrumental translation in verse 13a, "baptized *by* one Spirit," in which case, Petts argues, baptism *in* the Spirit is not in view here: this must be the work of the Spirit that incorporated a convert into the church. Dunn's appeal to the wider context of the New Testament is, writes Petts, a contradiction of the method Dunn has set out for biblical scholars, whereby each author should first be analyzed individually. However, Petts admits that if the immediate context is ignored then Dunn could be right to translate *en* as "in." In that case the appeal to a wider context allows a retranslation of *eis* (normally "into"), for if *en* means "in" at Matthew 3:11, then *eis* there certainly does not mean "into": John's baptismal candidates had already repented, so their baptism would not take them "into" repentance.[17]

Petts' arguments in this section are ill-founded. His claim that an instrumental use of *en* in 1 Corinthians 12:13a makes it "evident that it is the Spirit who is the baptizer, whereas in BHS [Baptism in the Holy Spirit] as understood by Pentecostals it is Jesus who is the baptizer"[18]

---

16. Admittedly, 1 Cor 12:13c could have no initiatory connotation at all but refer to repeated later Corinthian experiences of the Spirit. While the implication of the metaphor might support this interpretation—land needs to be continually watered, as do animals—the aorist tense, mirroring *ebaptithēmen*, and the overall poetic symmetry of the phrases argue against this.

17. NIV and NRSV both have "for" in Matt 3:11a. Actually, Dunn had already met this argument: New Testament baptism was "the Rubicon step of commitment without which faith and repentance were dead" (Dunn, *Baptism*, 128 n. 40). In other words, John's baptism *was* into repentance in the sense that until his listeners were baptized their repentance remained only embryonic.

18. Petts, "Baptism in the Holy Spirit," 80.

confuses the instrument of an action with its agent.[19] This confusion is understandable, for it is aided in the English language by our frequent use of "by" to denote both instrument and agent with the passive voice of a verb (e.g., compare "this book was written *by* me" with "this book was written *by* hand": in the first, "me" is the agent—the person who performs the action; in the second, "hand" is the instrument—the means by which I perform the action). Sometimes in English the confusion is mitigated by our use of other prepositions (so for example "this book was written *with* a laptop"), but in New Testament Greek there is rarely this uncertainty. With a passive verb, *en* plus the dative (or a prepositionless dative) in this context normally signifies an instrument;[20] *hupo* ("by") plus the genitive signifies an agent.[21] So in 1 Corinthians 12:13, where we have *en*, not *hupo*, the Spirit is unlikely to be the agent: the one who performs the action. The Spirit here is probably the instrument: the means by which the baptizing was performed. To say that the Holy Spirit is the instrument leaves the action without a stated agent, without a baptizer. But this is not a difficulty, for in the Bible the "divine passive" is common. In other words, the baptizer is not mentioned but is understood to be God. The clause then indicates that "we all" in Corinth were baptized *by* God (the agent) *with* one Spirit (God's chosen instrument) *into* one body. As a common meaning of *baptizō* ("baptize") was "immerse," then this clause might well indicate further that the way the agent (God) used the instrument (the Spirit) was as an immersing instrument: the Corinthians were immersed by God in one Spirit in order to bring them into one body.[22]

19. This is a common misunderstanding among Pentecostals. See Ervin, *Conversion-Initiation*, 99; Hunter, *Spirit Baptism*, 40; Holdcroft, *Holy Spirit*, 131; Horton, *What the Bible Says*, 214.

20. There are New Testament exceptions (e.g., Matt 23:5). However, in Paul's nearby use of *baptizō* . . . *en* . . . *eis* (1 Cor 10:2; "baptize in/by/with . . . into"), *en* (x2) clearly does not introduce the agents. It may be instrumental or locative, but as two other locative prepositions have been used of the cloud and the sea in the previous verse, *en* may well be instrumental in verse 2.

21. Wenham, *Elements of New Testament Greek*, 69–70, 245; Moule, *Idiom Book of New Testament Greek*, 44, 77. Thus, with reference to Petts' example taken from the context, 1 Cor 12:9 means in effect, "to another, faith [is given by God (agent)] by means of [instrument] the same Spirit."

22. However, it must be admitted that the picture is rather complicated. Many New Testament verbs used in the context of Spirit reception (e.g., "pour out," "fall upon," "come upon," "descend upon") suggest that this may have been viewed primarily as an effusion from above rather than (or as well as?) an immersion. If this is the case, then *baptizō en pneumati* should probably be translated "baptize *with* the Spirit" rather than

Petts' suggestion that *eis* need not be translated "into," based on a comparison with Matthew 3:11, is also weak. A more useful comparison than with Matthew would be Paul's own other uses of *baptizō eis* (usually "baptize into"). For Paul, one might have been baptized "into" Christ (Rom 6:3a; Gal 3:27), Christ's death (Rom 6:3b; cf. 6:4), Paul's name (1 Cor 1:13, 15), Moses (1 Cor 10:2), or one body (1 Cor 12:13). While the connotations may differ from passage to passage, the idea seems to be that of entering into a new relationship with or conformity with. Thus to be baptized "into" Christ or Paul was to belong to Christ or Paul (Gal 3:27–29; 1 Cor 1:12); to be baptized "into" Christ's death was to be conformed to that death (Rom 6:5); and, possibly, the Israelites' baptism "into" Moses was their entry into a new relationship with him whereby he, instead of Pharaoh, was their king.[23] A similar connotation would plausibly fit the context of 1 Corinthians 12:13—the Corinthians' being baptized (by God) in or with the Spirit had brought them into a new relationship with the one body. This coheres precisely with Paul's evident interest in verses 12 and 14 (the many varied parts of the body belong to the one united body) and easily justifies the translation of *eis* as "into" in verse 13. In summary, Dunn's understanding of this verse is more convincing than that of Petts. Paul referred to a baptism by God with or in the Spirit that effected a new relationship with and participation in the one body of Christ.

Summary

I took 1 Corinthians 12:13 as a test case, to see whether in this instance those Pentecostals who argue against Dunn's exegesis are able to do so successfully. It is clear that in this case they cannot. Although

---

"baptize *in* the Spirit." On the other hand, the common phrase "filled with the Spirit" coheres well with the idea of immersion, and in the close context of 1 Cor 12:13, 1 Cor 10:2 states that "all into Moses were baptized in the cloud and in the sea." The Israelites, with walls of water on either side of them, passed through the sea in a metaphorical immersion (cf. 1 Cor 10:1). So too their experience of the cloud was of immersion more than effusion (cf. Ps 105:39). It is thus not easy to be certain whether to translate *en* in 1 Cor 12:13a as "in" or "with."

23. So, tentatively, Moo, *Epistle to the Romans*, 360 n. 42. Dunn (*Baptism*, 126) and Fee (*First Epistle to the Corinthians*, 445) disagree with this, Dunn commenting that such a new relationship and loyalty would be depicted by *baptisma eis to onoma tou Mōuseōs* ("baptism into the name of Moses"; Dunn, *Baptism*, 126 n. 31). However, they offer no alternative.

1 Corinthians 12:13 refers specifically to incorporation into Christ's body, the church, rather than into Christ, it supports Dunn's thesis that for Paul receiving the Spirit, which in this verse he called being given one Spirit to drink and being baptized with one Spirit, was so intimately tied up with coming to Christ and his church that it would be inconceivable for Paul that a Christian would not yet have received the Spirit. Paul's pneumatology is indeed here "soteriological" and supports neither a later reception of the Spirit nor a complex of two receptions for different purposes. What has not yet been indicated is whether Paul perhaps wrote of two Spirit receptions elsewhere: an initial one that incorporated into Christ and his church, and a possibly later one that empowered. To answer this question would require a much fuller survey of Paul's words, and it is not my intention to offer that in this book. Suffice it to say that Paul did not.[24]

DUNN, PENTECOSTALS, AND PAUL

One might expect all the Pentecostals under review to have joined Ervin and Petts in mounting a fierce counter-attack against Dunn's reading of Paul, in order to preserve a distinctively Pentecostal reading of Paul. However, as I mentioned in the introduction to this chapter, they have not. In what appears on the surface to be a surprise move, apparently unforeseen by Dunn in 1970, several largely and unashamedly agree with his exegesis of Paul.[25] We will consider their individual responses briefly below.

Roger Stronstad

Not surprisingly, in his books about Luke's pneumatology, Stronstad makes no comment about Dunn's exegesis of Paul as such. However, his implicit response is one of agreement, for he writes, "Paul knows that all Christians have the Spirit (Rom 8:9)."[26] This does not mean that Stronstad would accept, with Dunn, that Romans 8 is "one of the NT's most crush-

---

24. For further discussion of Pentecostal arguments against Dunn regarding Paul's letters, see my "Pentecostal Responses: Pauline Literature."

25. Janet Everts disagrees with Dunn in her consideration of 2 Cor 1:21–22 and Eph 1:13–14. See Everts, "Pauline Letters" and Dunn's reply in Dunn, "Baptism Again," 36–38.

26. Stronstad, *Charismatic Theology*, 68. So too 1 Cor 12:13 "references initiation-incorporation" (Stronstad, "On Being Baptized," 161).

ing denials of Pentecostal . . . teaching,"[27] for Stronstad's point, as I noted in chapter 2, is that Luke's pneumatology was distinctively different from that of Paul. What Luke meant by the term *to receive the Spirit* is different from what Paul meant. Thus, "there is no tension between the fact of the indwelling of the Holy Spirit in the life of every believer and an additional experience of receiving the prophetic or charismatic gift of the Spirit."[28]

James Shelton

Shelton's response is remarkably similar to Stronstad's, though somewhat more detailed. He agrees with Stronstad that Luke actually needs to be "contrasted" with Paul. In relation to conversion, he too refers to Romans 8:9.[29] Later, with reference to Dunn, he makes the more detailed point that the differences between Paul and Luke can be accounted for by the different purposes for which the two men were writing. In Romans 8:9 specifically, Paul was addressing an "ontological" question: "How is one a Christian?" Luke, specifically in his account of Pentecost, was asking a practical question: "How do we witness?" Dunn's use, for example, of Romans 8:9 as part of the logic with which to bolster his reading of the Samaritan episode in Acts 8, "does not respect the redactional motives of Luke and Paul, which are *not* completely interchangeable."[30]

Robert Menzies

Menzies' earlier book, *The Development of Early Christian Pneumatology*, is subtitled *with Special Reference to Luke-Acts*. Nonetheless, he does include a section on the pneumatology of Paul. In this section, he describes Paul's pneumatology as "soteriological," thereby implicitly agreeing with Dunn's viewpoint. Indeed, his first footnote in the section recom-

---

27. Dunn, *Baptism*, 148.

28. Stronstad, *Charismatic Theology*, 68.

29. Shelton, *Mighty in Word and Deed*, 5.

30. Ibid., 127; quotation from 149 n. 11; italics original. Cf. ibid., 160: "Luke does not define the relationship of conversion and the Holy Spirit as clearly as Paul does. His attention is usually upon the relationship of the Holy Spirit and witness, a subject on which he is much clearer." Not all would agree with Shelton. For Twelftree, the detail Luke offers in otherwise minor accounts like Acts 19:1–6 causes him to conclude that "it is Luke's interest in establishing the reception of the Spirit as critical for being a disciple that has motivated his writing in such detail" (Twelftree, *People of the Spirit*, 94).

mends another portion of Dunn's work as "a good overview of Paul's
soteriology."[31]

Menzies' characterization of Pauline pneumatology as soteriological and Lukan pneumatology as prophetic means of course that he views
each as "acutely" distinct from the other.[32] To those who find such a diversity of viewpoint theologically or historically improbable, he wisely
replies:

a. "it is tragic when, in the name of biblical inspiration, legitimate
    theological diversity within the canon is repudiated;"

b. "assumptions concerning the extent to which Luke was in-
    fluenced by Paul must be judged in the light of the evidence
    we have available to us, not on speculation of what might
    have been."[33]

Gordon Fee

I did not have sections on Fee in earlier chapters. He has not engaged with
Dunn over Pentecostal Spirit baptism.[34] Also, Fee's writing on Pauline
pneumatology is vastly greater than his work on Lukan pneumatology.
It is therefore not surprising that he interacts significantly with Dunn on
the former subject and hardly at all on the latter. His main relevant work
is his excellent *God's Empowering Presence*. In it he makes occasional
references to Lukan pneumatology, which he too sees as fundamentally
similar to that of Paul.[35] He notes Dunn's comment in *Baptism* about
Paul's writings being an embarrassment to Pentecostals,[36] but clearly
finds nothing embarrassing there himself. He is in broad agreement with
Dunn about the significance of Spirit reception in Paul, even though he
finds plenty about which to disagree with Dunn, perhaps most notably

31. Menzies, *Development*, 282 n. 1.

32. Ibid., 318.

33. Menzies, "Distinctive Character of Luke's Pneumatology," 26, 27.

34. Mittelstadt includes Fee as the first name in his cataloging of the Pentecostal
debate sparked by Dunn's *Baptism*, but he acknowledges that in fact Fee did not engage
with that debate *directly*: only with the wider hermeneutical issues it raised (Mittelstadt,
Reading Luke-Acts, 49–50).

35. Fee, *God's Empowering Presence*, e.g., 35, 384; similarly Fee, *Galatians*, 107.

36. Fee, *God's Empowering Presence*, 10.

in their divergent views on Pauline discussions about the relations between "flesh" and "S/spirit," and between "law" and "S/spirit."[37]

Max Turner (1996)

Turner's *Holy Spirit and Spiritual Gifts* contains two chapters on Paul. On the subject of Spirit reception, he is in close agreement with Dunn, to whose *Baptism* he refers approvingly in his exegesis of 2 Corinthians 3:16–17 and Galatians 4:6.[38] He draws upon Dunn's work to reach the conclusion that Paul "cannot elucidate receiving the Spirit in terms of 'Confirmation,' or some other second blessing, e.g., 'baptism in the Holy Spirit' (as understood by classical Pentecostals), because for Paul the Spirit is essentially the Spirit of the new covenant. Without this gift there is no new creation, no new heart or new spirit, no 'life,' and no new covenant relationship."[39] Turner's only significant disagreement with Dunn lies in another area of Pauline pneumatology: they do not concur over the extent to which Paul in effect blurred the distinctions between the Spirit and the risen Christ.[40]

Dunn's Reading of Pentecostalism

That Fee and Turner should agree with Dunn is not surprising. Perhaps more surprising is that Stronstad, Shelton, and Menzies should do so. A noteworthy paradox is at work here. On the one hand, every time Dunn exegetes a Pauline passage to show that Spirit reception is what makes one a Christian, he declares that the passage destroys the Pentecostals' case completely.[41] On the other hand, many of his Pentecostal respondents happily concur with his overall exegesis of Paul, or at least with that of Romans 8 (when this is the only Pauline text they mention). They do so without any hint of conceding to Dunn, or any suggestion that their views have been swayed by his contribution. This obvious paradox leads to a suspicion: Dunn's exegesis of Paul's may be sound enough, but has he actually misread Pentecostalism?

---

37. See, e.g., Fee, *God's Empowering Presence*, 511–38.
38. Turner, *Holy Spirit and Spiritual Gifts*, 117, 122–23 n. 17.
39. Ibid., 118.
40. Ibid., 130–33.
41. Dunn, *Baptism*, e.g., 107, 123, 135.

In his conclusion he states: "Most Pentecostals recognize the force of Rom. 8.9 and agree that to be a Christian one must have received the Spirit in some sense."[42] In the light of his earlier studies, this statement raises a serious question. If Dunn accepts that most Pentecostals recognize from Romans 8:9 that all Christians have the Spirit "in some sense," how can he declare that Romans 8 is "one of the most crushing denials"[43] of Pentecostalism? What he admits in his conclusion (and only then), he implicitly denies earlier through such dismissive statements. In fact, every time he claims that such passages destroy Pentecostal doctrine, he is making the same implicit, and highly inaccurate, declaration: Pentecostals deny any reception of the Spirit other than an empowering subsequent to conversion. Only in his conclusion does he concede otherwise.

Admittedly, when addressing Romans 8:9 directly Dunn only attacks what he calls the "crude" Pentecostal view: "that conversion is a matter of receiving Christ and Spirit-baptism of receiving the Spirit."[44] At this point at least he seems to recognize that there might be a more sophisticated version of Pentecostalism, which is able to give full weight to this verse. However, elsewhere he makes no such concession. The following sentence does not suggest that it is describing only a crude "minority" Pentecostal view: "The Pentecostal attempt to evade the NT emphasis by distinguishing the acceptance of Jesus at conversion from the later gift of the Spirit is in fact a departure from NT teaching."[45]

What this means in effect is that despite some minor concessions to the contrary, Dunn claims that Pentecostals fail to give any weight to Paul's soteriological pneumatology. Their view is "crude": Jesus comes at conversion; the Spirit only comes at the convert's Spirit baptism. To verify that at least some Pentecostals hold this crude view, he offers three pieces of evidence.

a. Appeals are frequently made to "receive Jesus" in "popular evangelism."

b. Howard Ervin in a footnote writes, "In the 'new birth' we first receive Jesus . . . In the baptism in the Spirit we receive power."

42. Ibid., 170.
43. Ibid., 148.
44. Ibid.
45. Ibid., 95.

c. A Blessed Trinity Society pamphlet has the words, "Once we have accepted the Lord Jesus Christ, there is a further step . . . that is the acceptance of the Gift of the Holy Spirit."[46]

This is scant evidence.

a. Popular evangelism cannot be expected to announce every nuance of an evangelist's soteriology or pneumatology.

b. Ervin's understanding must be gleaned from more than a single footnote. Ervin devotes a whole chapter of the same work to an exposition of John 20:19–23 to make precisely the point that the apostles were born again *by receiving the Spirit*.[47]

c. As with appeals in popular evangelism, so with pamphlets. Also, the Blessed Trinity Society, founded in 1960, served the charismatic movement of the time in the older denominations.[48] The charismatic movement and its "children" have been characterized by as wide divergences in their theology as they display in their denominational identities. Furthermore, the early charismatic movement's understandings of Christian initiation fluctuated greatly, so that Michael Harper, for instance, could write in favor of a doctrine of subsequence in 1965, but appear to deny it in 1974.[49] The Blessed Trinity Society cannot be permitted to speak for classical Pentecostalism.

There is far more evidence that classical Pentecostalism has always taught (even if not entirely consistently) that all Christians have the Spirit. When Pentecostalism first emerged, it drew heavily on the writings of R. A. Torrey, described by Bruner as one of the most influential figures in the pre-history of Pentecostalism: "a kind of John the Baptist figure for later international Pentecostalism."[50] Writing in 1898, Torrey declared, "*Every true believer has the Holy Spirit. But not every believer*

---

46. Ibid., 95, 93 n. 5. The reference to Ervin's work is to Ervin, *These Are Not Drunken*, 93 n. 15.

47. Ervin, *These Are Not Drunken*, ch. III, e.g., "Jesus imparted new spiritual life to His followers by breathing the Holy Spirit into them" (ibid., 31).

48. Irish, "Blessed Trinity Society."

49. See Petts, "Baptism in the Holy Spirit," 34–35.

50. Bruner, *Theology of the Holy Spirit*, 45.

has the Baptism with the Holy Spirit."[51] This doctrine was adopted by early Pentecostalism. In 1911, an article in the *Upper Room* periodical, published in Los Angeles by classical Pentecostals, acknowledged that there was "a teaching in some Pentecostal quarters that the Holy Ghost has not been received at all, except by those who has [*sic*] received the full Pentecostal baptism." This doctrine the article in question went on to repudiate emphatically: "of course, we cannot subscribe to this for one moment."[52] In 1937, Myer Pearlman wrote that "one cannot be a Christian without having the Spirit, which is the same as being indwelt by the Spirit."[53] Dalton's research into the Pentecostal movement, published in 1945, concluded: "Pentecostal theology does not deny that a non-Pentecostal has the Holy Spirit. It teaches that all have the Holy Spirit within their hearts from conversion on."[54] Ralph Riggs wrote in 1949 that "they who are Christ's have the Spirit of Christ,"[55] and that "the Holy Spirit comes into one's heart at conversion."[56] The same view was held by Harold Horton (1946) and by Ernest Williams (1953).[57] This understanding continues in more recent decades. Stanley Horton and Thomas Holdcroft both clearly hold the view.[58]

Later analyses of Pentecostalism offer a similar verdict. Bruner writes that "there is a difference in Pentecostal conviction . . . between simply *receiving* the Spirit (which happens to all Christians in some measure at conversion) and *fully* receiving him" and that "it is granted that all believers are somehow, or in a sense, indwelt by the Spirit, or are at the very least affected by him."[59] J. Rodman Williams implies that this is the normal position within Pentecostalism.[60] Harold Hunter rues the uncertainty that he detects among Pentecostals at a popular level on

---

51. Quoted by ibid., 335; italics his.

52. Quoted in Hunter, *Spirit Baptism* (2009), 223.

53. Quoted by Bruner, *Theology of the Holy Spirit*, 70 n.18.

54. Quoted by Petts, "Baptism in the Holy Spirit," 10.

55. Quoted by Holdcroft, *Holy Spirit*, 129.

56. Quoted with an unsurprising exclamation mark by Dunn, *Baptism*, 113 n. 29. Riggs is also praised by Dunn for an "entirely orthodox interpretation of [Romans] 8.9" (Dunn, *Baptism*, 149).

57. See Bruner, *Theology of the Holy Spirit*, 70 n. 18.

58. Horton, *What the Bible Says*, 132–33; Holdcroft, *Holy Spirit*, 76–78, 107, 132.

59. Bruner, *Theology of the Holy Spirit*, 60, 70; italics his.

60. Williams, "Baptism in the Holy Spirit," 42.

this subject, blaming the movement's "theological illiteracy," but claims that "whenever a Pentecostalist embarks onto theological terrain, he or she invariably affirms the truth that all Christians know the indwelling presence of the Holy Spirit."[61] David Pawson, who himself teaches a form of subsequence,[62] repeatedly criticizes Pentecostals for believing in two Spirit receptions.[63] Julian Ward briefly records this aspect of Pentecostal belief: "Pentecostals . . . distinguish between the indwelling of the Holy Spirit as the source of saving faith . . . and the outpouring of the Spirit that empowers."[64] Menzies, commenting on what Pentecostals and other Christians have in common, writes "together, we affirm that every Christian receives the life-giving and indwelling Spirit. There is no Christian without the Spirit."[65] Admittedly, the picture is not entirely consistent. Keith Warrington writes that "traditionally, Pentecostals have separated the Spirit from the act of salvation to such an extent that it has been difficult to deduce his role in salvation."[66] However, given the weight of testimony and analysis already presented, Warrington's emerges as something of a lone voice.

This survey reveals that the overwhelming majority of written Pentecostal teaching throughout its history has made room for Paul's soteriological pneumatology. Dunn's criticisms have been misplaced.

Conclusion

It is time now to bring together various strands of thought that have engaged our thinking throughout this chapter so far. The first is that when certain Pentecostals try to mount a challenge to Dunn's exegesis of the Pauline literature relating to Spirit reception, they fail. Another strand is that, in fact, many Pentecostals have simply not attempted to argue against Dunn here. They explicitly agree with Dunn's reading of Paul on these texts, and do so without either embarrassment (despite Dunn's claims) or hesitation. These Pentecostal scholars (Stronstad, Turner in 1980, Shelton, and Menzies—and I) can all agree with Dunn concerning

61. Hunter, *Spirit Baptism* (2009), 223, 225.
62. Pawson, *Normal Christian Birth*, 291–93.
63. Ibid., 4, 283–84, 323.
64. Ward, "Pentecostalist Theology," 504.
65. Menzies, "Luke's Understanding," 122.
66. Warrington, *Pentecostal Theology*, 128.

Paul while disagreeing with him concerning Luke simply because we do not identify Paul's thinking as closely with Luke's as Dunn does. This is not to say that we necessarily see frank contradiction between the two New Testament authors. Rather, we see at least noteworthy distinctions in pneumatology. A third strand that has emerged is that Pentecostalism has always recognized that all Christians have the Spirit, even before their Spirit baptism. I am not claiming that this has been completely consistent (see for example Warrington's demurring and Harold Hunter's concerns, referred to above) and I am certainly not claiming that this traditional Pentecostal view has come about through a scholarly nuanced reading of Luke and Paul. One might, if taking a pejorative view of Pentecostal Bible reading, say that it has come about almost by accident. But that is probably too harsh. Rather, the Lukan data and the Pauline data (not to mention data from elsewhere in the Bible) have been agglomerated in an unnuanced fashion, and the concoction that has arisen from these ingredients has been the two-stage Spirit reception that is implicit in the Pentecostal doctrine of subsequence and explicit in many of its expositions. Current Pentecostal New Testament scholars are claiming that very similar conclusions are reached when, in the place of untutored intuitive Bible reading, nuanced lines of biblical scholarship are pursued.

THE LUKAN PAUL AND THE EPISTOLARY PAUL

Thus Stronstad, Shelton, and Menzies rightly indicate that there are substantial differences between Lukan and Pauline pneumatologies, which affect their understandings of Spirit reception. How these differences can be recognized and maintained when integrated as part of the process of forming an overall New Testament view of Spirit reception is a matter that we will come to later in this chapter. First, however, we have to face a prior complication. Paul appears in Luke's second volume, and the character called Paul whom we find there does not sound precisely like the Paul we know from his letters: hence the terms "Lukan Paul" and "epistolary Paul" in the section title. Differences are apparent in a number of areas that have engaged scholarly minds, but for our purposes a key "problem area" is Acts 19:2.

The Case of Acts 19:2

Acts 19:2 presents intriguing questions for those, Pentecostal or otherwise, who see variations between Luke's and Paul's ideas concerning the Spirit's role in conversion. The crux of the matter is that Paul asked a question here that was compatible with Luke's view of the Spirit's role, but incompatible with the epistolary Paul's view. The Paul who wrote Romans 8:9 simply would not have asked the question, for his logic would inform him that these Ephesians, evidently lacking the Spirit, were not believers, however highly they might speak of John the Baptist or even of Apollos. For this Paul, the question was a "non-question." There are various ways in which this intriguing matter can be addressed. For those who have a low view of the historicity of Acts, it presents no problem: the account is Lukan, pure and simple. Luke redacted his sources, or simply created the material, in order to further his portrayal of the church, its activities, and its beliefs.[67] The perspective of the historical Paul is irrelevant to the account. I do not share this view of Luke's history writing. Nor, I suspect, would many Pentecostals. In contrast, for Dunn, there is no problem, for there is no distinction to be drawn between Luke's and Paul's pneumatologies at this point. So Dunn informs us that while the wording of the account as a whole is Lukan, the phrasing of the question itself is undoubtedly Pauline.[68] It is those who regard Luke-Acts as both historically accurate and pneumatologically distinct from Paul's letters for whom this poses the sharpest challenge.

Possible solutions, which are not mutually exclusive, include regarding the question as, on the one hand, charitable, or on the other as suspicious.[69] It may have been *ad hominem*:[70] Paul knew full well that the Ephesians were not believers, but *they* thought they were, and so he "spoke their language" to communicate with them effectively. These are all possible, and are better solutions than the one offered by Stronstad, who cross-refers to the epistolary Paul, and Romans 8:9 specifically, as

---

67. This view is not rare among New Testament scholars (for discussion of Lukan historiography, see Witherington, *Acts*, 15–39). Among those Pentecostal and charismatic authors taking an interest in the charismatic pneumatology of Luke-Acts, this tendency is evident in Twelftree, *People of the Spirit*. See, e.g., his references to Luke's account of Pentecost (ibid., 65–71).

68. Dunn, *Acts*, 253, 255.

69. Dunn, *Baptism*, 84, 86.

70. Turner, "Luke and the Spirit," 175.

evidence that Paul in Acts 19:2 was not referring to a soteriological reception of the Spirit.[71] In effect, according to Stronstad, Paul knew of two
Spirit receptions: the one implied in Romans 8:9; and a later charismatic
one that he referred to in Acts 19:2. The problem with this suggestion
is that if Paul did conceive of two Spirit receptions in the processes of
conversion and early Christian growth, one would expect evidence of
that to emerge in his letters, and it does not, however hard Pentecostals
have tried to seek it.

More satisfactory is the conclusion of Turner in 1980: while Paul
no doubt did ask a question that sought to clarify "where these disciples
stood" with regard to Christian discipleship, the precise wording of the
question as recorded is Lukan, not Pauline.[72] This is not to say that the
account is unhistorical—simply that Luke reported it in his own words.
After all, the account does not fall within one of the "we/us" passages in
Acts, and so we do not surmise that Luke was present to hear Paul's question. The whole incident was reported to him. Also, Luke wrote Acts perhaps twenty or thirty years after this incident occurred.[73] Furthermore,
as with Luke's records of apostolic and other speeches in Acts,[74] there is
every reason to believe that Luke did not set out to record conversations
in full, but to offer brief highlights that communicated their central features.[75] All these factors support the conclusion that we would be most
unlikely to have Paul's precise words. Luke knew that the conversation
occurred along these lines: he recorded it in his own words. The words

71. Stronstad, *Charismatic Theology*, 68.

72. Turner, "Luke and the Spirit," 175. Elbert's perceptive analysis of the wording of
certain questions in Luke-Acts further demonstrates the likelihood of this question's
wording being Lukan (Elbert, "Observation on Luke's Composition," especially 107).

73. The events recorded in Acts 19 occurred in perhaps AD 54–55 (Witherington,
Acts, 84). We do not know when Acts was written, but perhaps between AD 75 and 85.
Even the theory that Acts was written immediately after the close of its narrative (AD
62?—see Wenham, *Redating Matthew, Mark & Luke*, xxvi, 225–29) places the writing
seven or eight years after the event.

74. For discussion of the speeches in Acts, see Witherington, *Acts*, 116–23. According
to Witherington, Luke's records of the speeches are "summaries": "a skeletal outline," put
"into his own words," with "perhaps some memorable phrases and stylistic features." In
these speeches, "certain Lukan stylistic traits and themes crop up regularly" (ibid., 117
and nn. 8, 9, 10).

75. Nobody would likely infer from Acts 6:2 ("The twelve . . . said") that the twelve
apostles chanted in unison, "It is not desirable for us . . . to serve at tables." Examples of
such summaries of conversations are numerous.

we read in Acts 19:2 reflect the linguistic preferences of Luke, not of the epistolary Paul.

A counter-argument to this suggestion that might be offered among Pentecostals is that the God who inspires Scripture would never allow such "discrepancy." Divine oversight of the process would supernaturally protect it from lapses of memory or transmission. I feel the force of that argument, but it is important to recognize Luke's own perception of how he came across his material. He did not receive it through visions and dreams (!), however much some of his characters might have gained divine insights this way. He resorted, with good reason, to the very human process of careful research (Luke 1:3). While divine superintendence is granted, the human limitations of Luke's research must be granted as well, according to his own testimony.

ANOTHER TEST CASE: JOHN 20:22

Turning now to the testimony of the Fourth Gospel, I again take a test case approach. John 20:22 is a text often used by Pentecostals to argue that the disciples were already regenerate before Pentecost, through Jesus' life-giving insufflation of the Holy Spirit into them. They were then baptized in the Spirit at Pentecost as recorded in Acts, and in these disciples' spiritual history it emerges both that baptism in the Spirit is not identical to regeneration, and that the Spirit is involved in both, working in the process of regeneration (as in John 3:3–8) and again, in a different way, in Spirit baptism. Among the debaters round our table, Ervin follows this line of reasoning.[76]

In his chapter on the "Johannine Pentecost," Dunn dismisses two other ways of reading John 20:22. It cannot merely be a proleptic pronouncement by Jesus pointing forward to a Spirit baptism yet to come ("Receive the Spirit at some time in the future"), for this "is an unsupported speculation which does too little justice to the text."[77] Equally, this cannot be John's account of "Pentecost," tempting as the suggestion is. In other words, this cannot be the moment when Jesus' promise of the arrival of the Paraclete (John 14–16) is fulfilled. This is because that promise is for a "sending" from the Father as well as the Son (John 14:26;

---

76. E.g., Ervin, *Spirit-Baptism*, chs. 3 and 4.

77. Dunn, *Baptism*, 178; so too Turner, *Holy Spirit and Spiritual Gifts*, 90–92.

15:26). It is a promise that will be fulfilled once Jesus has "gone away," and thus the Holy Spirit will be "another" Paraclete, to "replace" Jesus.[78]

Dunn thus finds himself straying perilously close to Pentecostal territory. He is to be admired for his honesty in exegesis when the temptation, as he admits, is to follow a reading more clearly at odds with the Pentecostal one set out above. He concedes that in the case of these first disciples, John knew of two initiating Spirit receptions: the regenerating one recorded by John at 20:22, and a further one that would fulfill the promises of chapters 14–16, but that John did not report. Dunn even concedes that this fits the chronology of Acts.[79] However, as Ervin notes,[80] Dunn agrees so fully with Pentecostal sentiments here that he is only able to part company with them at this point by appealing to the uniqueness of this particular event. It is unrepeatable for three reasons.

a. Jesus' ministry marked the covenantal turning point when "eternal life was essentially a matter of believing in him."

b. It was only now, as a result of Jesus' immediately preceding death and resurrection, that the Spirit could be given (John 7:39).

c. The wording of John 20:22, recalling Genesis 2:7, indicates a unique new creation at this point.[81]

Naturally, Ervin regards this as unacceptable, partly because he continues to assert that John's and Luke's accounts can be taken in tandem, and partly because he denies that the first disciples should be regarded as unique: "to postulate a transition period in salvation history between the resurrection and Pentecost is to consign the apostolic community to a dispensational limbo."[82]

In contrast, Turner agrees in almost every respect with Dunn. He is closer, in fact, to Dunn's position concerning John than he is concerning Luke-Acts. He notes only two areas of disagreement. The first is that

78. Dunn, *Baptism*, 177.

79. Ibid. Unlike the Pentecostal reading introduced in the first paragraph of this section, Dunn has no need to alloy John's testimony with that of Luke. His conclusion thus far is drawn purely from John.

80. Ervin, *Spirit-Baptism*, 19–20 n. 36.

81. Dunn, *Baptism*, 179–80; quotation from 179. Dunn actually lists four reasons, but his fourth (ibid., 181) is essentially a repetition of his first.

82. Ervin, *Conversion-Initiation*, 137.

Dunn is wrong to regard John 20:22 alone as the point at which these first disciples found new life in Christ. He is able to present plentiful evidence that, as in Luke's portrayal, these followers had tasted new life through the Spirit-enabled ministry of Jesus prior to the latter's death and resurrection (e.g., John 15:3).[83] The second note of disagreement with Dunn concerns the reason that the two-stage Spirit reception for these disciples is historically unrepeatable. For Turner, it cannot happen again because Jesus is now absent through exaltation: never again can people walk with the incarnate Jesus, learn from him, and taste new life in this unique way before receiving the Paraclete. Now, it must always and naturally be the arrival of the Paraclete that will both fulfill the promises of John 14–16 for an Advocate who will guide them in their ministries and present their case to an unbelieving world and also fulfill the promises of new life presented to Nicodemus in John 3.[84]

Critique of Dunn and Turner

Neither Dunn nor Turner demonstrates his case from the evidence John offers them. Rather, they merely assert their similar positions. Turner's reasoning is the easier to counter-argue: while Jesus will not lead people again into new life through his incarnate ministry, his followers who are themselves enabled by the Paraclete's work in them now perform the same function. People come to eternal life, John might declare, as Jesus' post-exaltation followers advocate the message of this new life through Jesus. If people today are able to gain the same revelation of God's truth through this channel as the Samaritan villagers did, for instance (John 4:39–42), then there is no reason why they should not receive from the exalted Jesus the insufflation of the Spirit that is equivalent to that in John 20:22. If, according to John, this can be chronologically separated from the reception of the Paraclete in the first disciples' lives, there is no reason why the same should not apply today.

Dunn's reasoning requires a rather more careful response. It is undeniably the case that Jesus' incarnate ministry was the turning point that introduced, through his death and resurrection, the replacement of the Mosaic covenant (John 1:17). It is also beyond doubt that the living water of the Spirit was unavailable until after these events (John 7:39), even if, as

83. Turner, *Holy Spirit and Spiritual Gifts*, 98–99. Thomas agrees (Thomas, "Celebration and Engagement," 22).

84. Turner, *Holy Spirit and Spiritual Gifts*, 101–2.

Turner observes, Jesus' hearers could already taste spiritual life through Jesus' Spirit-enabled teaching (John 3:34; 4:10, 15; 6:63). However, these unrepeatable events had occurred *before* John 20:22. To argue, admittedly, from John's silence, there is nothing essentially unrepeatable in salvation history or church history about the disciples' lives between their recorded Spirit reception (John 20:22) and their unrecorded Paraclete reception. Dunn seems to be aware of this counter-argument, for after all his careful exegesis of John's words, he has to resort at the last minute to a conflation of John's testimony with Acts chronology, and argue that the "transition period between the dispensations" lasted all the way through to Pentecost. But he offers no unalloyed evidence from John to support this assertion.[85]

Even if my counter-arguments to Dunn and Turner at this point prove unconvincing, it is instructive for Pentecostalism that John, alone among the New Testament authors studied, portrayed two different receptions of the Spirit in the lives of those first disciples, evidently with different functions in their lives (for the early disciples who received the Paraclete were already regenerate).

LISTENING TO LUKE, PAUL, AND JOHN TOGETHER

As I wrote at the beginning of this chapter, Pentecostals, like any other Christians who take the teaching of the Bible seriously, want to listen to its whole testimony in forming their doctrines and setting their practices. Once the individual voices have been heard, their various perspectives and emphases must be brought together. We naturally assume that the God who has superintended the writing of these Scriptures will ensure that the resultant sound is a symphony, not a cacophony. Once the overall New Testament "chorus" has been heard, the task of applying this to today's situations can begin (and wise Christians will in the process listen to the ways in which those same Scriptures have been heard by other Christians down the centuries).

Menzies and Turner

As Dunn finds no significant differences between Luke, Paul, and John concerning Spirit reception, he does not have any detailed section on how their voices can be heard together. Therefore this part of the de-

---

85. Dunn, *Baptism*, 181.

bate is initiated by Menzies, with Dunn's "part" being taken by Turner.[86] Menzies only discusses Luke and Paul; Turner studies John as well.

While referring to the impact of Dunn's *Baptism* on Pentecostal thinking and writing, Menzies actually interacts in his relevant chapter with the work of Fee.[87] In contrast to Fee's position, Menzies emphasizes that Luke's view of the Spirit is sharply distinguishable from Paul's, although ultimately reconcilable. Luke's charismatic pneumatology, which Menzies understands to be specifically prophetic, creates the conceptual foundation for the Pentecostal doctrine of subsequence. To the two counter-arguments that he anticipates—that God would not allow such diversity of viewpoint in the Bible, and that Luke and Paul, as companions in ministry, would be bound to have views in close approximation—he responds by observing, as I noted earlier, that a belief in the Bible's God-given overall unity must not mask its human diversity, and that in fact Luke evidences ignorance of a range of distinctive Pauline doctrines.[88]

In response, Turner observes that Menzies has not actually set out a program for drawing an overall New Testament view of Spirit reception from the various New Testament voices. However, Turner assumes

---

86. Mittelstadt calls Turner a new "Dunn-like" conversation partner for the Pentecostals in this whole debate (Mittelstadt, *Reading Luke-Acts*, 60).

87. Menzies observes that Fee agrees largely with Dunn concerning the matters under debate, and describes Fee's critique of some older Pentecostal defenses of subsequence from Luke-Acts: they rested on inadequate hermeneutics, arguing from the analogy of Jesus' anointing or of Pentecost (both of which, Menzies concedes, are historically unique), or from the assumption that a few "proof texts" in Acts offer a historical precedent for today's Pentecostals, but failing to indicate that Luke intended these (Menzies, *Empowered for Witness*, 233–35). Menzies is unconcerned by these points, for, he observes, such readings of Luke-Acts as his and Stronstad's do not rest on these outdated hermeneutics. Rather, they indicate that Luke's pneumatology prevents reading Spirit reception passages in Luke-Acts soteriologically (ibid., 237). I am not sure that Menzies needs to cede so much ground to Fee. Luke's intention is to present Jesus' anointing as at least in part analogous to later ones. So Dunn notes, although, as Turner (1980) highlights, Jesus' anointing is in other important ways unique. That Luke intended to offer Jesus' anointing as in some ways analogous is evident from Acts 1:1, with its "Jesus began to do and teach." The implication is that the Spirit of Jesus on the disciples would enable Jesus through them to *continue* to do and teach as he had done earlier. Also, the day of Pentecost was offered as an analogy by Luke for further receptions (Acts 11:15–17). Although Menzies calls Stronstad to his side in his appeal to more "modern" hermeneutics, actually Stronstad's references to a transfer motif indicate that Stronstad is seeing the anointing on Jesus as analogous to that on the 120 (and thereby, by extension, to those on all Christ's subsequent followers).

88. Menzies, *Empowered for Witness*, 240–42.

that Menzies and similar Pentecostals want a simple addition: Paul's voice has supplied New Testament evidence for the arrival of the life-giving Spirit in initial conversion; Luke has offered similar evidence for the empowering work of the Spirit at a potentially later Spirit baptism. This Turner regards as unacceptable, for even on Menzies' reading Luke's and Paul's views are not sufficiently different from one another to be added together in this way: Paul believed all that Luke did, and more. Paul believed that the arrival of the Spirit was charismatic—and life-giving. There was no distinct subsequent charismatic work of the Spirit that could occur once Paul's conceived Spirit had come into someone's life. Of course, there could be the inception of an individual gift or an intensification of the Spirit's work, but that was not distinct enough for Paul to call it the arrival of the Spirit.[89]

Turner sees yet further problems with the Pentecostal articulation of Spirit baptism. In particular, Pentecostals are unable to offer a biblically founded distinction between the activity of the Spirit in regeneration and the activity of the Spirit in Spirit baptism. The argument that in the former the Spirit grants new life in Christ to the recipient, while in the latter the Spirit empowers the Christian's ministry for others is not biblically based, for according to Luke, Paul, and John *all* these activities of the Spirit are simply Christian developments of the Jewish concept of the Spirit of prophecy.[90]

One feels the force of Turner's thorough and careful argumentation. However, while it is strong, it is not invincible. On the first point, that there is no distinct "second" experience of the Spirit in the New Testament, only momentary intensifications and the inception of various gifts, we have testimony from both John and Luke that weakens Turner's claim. John did know of two receptions of the Spirit: one to regenerate and one to act in ways distinct from this (for, as I noted above, the arrival of the Paraclete to those first disciples would have come to regenerate people). Even if Dunn and Turner are right in claiming that John only knew of this prior to and including the day of Pentecost, this is an important recognition. A New Testament author could speak of different arrivals of the Spirit in those people: one cannot argue that no New Testament author knew of works of the Spirit distinct enough to articulate this as two different arrivals of the Spirit. Furthermore,

89. Turner, *Holy Spirit and Spiritual Gifts*, 152–55.
90. Ibid., 156.

neither Dunn nor Turner has provided evidence from John's writing that John could not have conceived of this distinction continuing beyond Pentecost. Luke, on the other hand, did not write of two Spirit receptions except in the case of Jesus (Luke 3:22; Acts 2:33). However, as I discussed in chapter 3, he wrote of what I have called the "prior works of the Spirit" in someone's life before what he called that person's reception of the Spirit. And it was Luke, more than John (for Luke had the opportunity in Acts), who described the effect of *this* reception of the Spirit in recipients' lives. It was not for regeneration (to use John's term), but for charismatic equipping.

With respect to the second point made by Turner, that all three authors simply offered "Christianized" developments of one unitary Jewish concept—the Spirit of prophecy, Turner seems to have imposed a "Spirit of prophecy grid" on his reading of these various authors, thereby diminishing the distinctives of their voices. One fears that the historical context has been exegeted somewhat to the detriment of the texts themselves. It has already become apparent that these authors used the same terms in different ways, reflecting different ways of viewing the Spirit's work. That *all* the Spirit's activities could be included under the banner heading of "Spirit of prophecy" did not preclude the possibility that *some* of those activities were necessary for conversion to Christ, while *others* were not.

One also feels the force of Turner's complaint that Pentecostals cannot offer a clear distinction between the activity of the Spirit in regeneration and the activity of the Spirit in Spirit baptism, when he refers not to the question of whether this can be biblically founded, but to whether it can be evidenced from observation of today's churches. He regards Pentecostal experience as an unreliable guide, for, he notes, non-Pentecostal churches can be found where people are as "spiritual" and as spiritually gifted as in Pentecostal churches, if not more so.[91] This observation may happen to be correct, but his point is not convincing, on two counts. First, his claim is not empirically verifiable or falsifiable. Also, the same claim, very sadly, may be made about Christianity as a whole: there are people who do not own Christ who may be as gifted or as morally upright as those who do own Christ, if not more so. Turner would have done better to resort only to the "before-and-after" testimo-

91. Ibid., 163.

nies of individuals.[92] Many of these would be verifiable in terms of their outward behavior: and the testimony of some is of a distinct empowering subsequent to initial conversion to Christ. Of course, by no means all Christians, or all Pentecostals, have this testimony. But the fact that some do means that Pentecostals are not at a loss in articulating a distinct subsequent work of the Spirit. Again, arguments can be had about the meaning of "salvation"—in Pentecostal discourse as well as in Luke's writings—but distinctions can be drawn between coming to saving faith in Christ and being empowered charismatically by the Spirit.

More generally, Turner finds the Pentecostal articulation of Christian beginnings and life unsatisfactory, because of the sheer variety in current Christian practice and experience: not only do many outside the Pentecostal churches experience spiritual gifts, but various spiritual gifts are themselves hard to differentiate from natural abilities; and while the Pentecostal testimony of a subsequent empowering undoubtedly exists, many people testify to a gradual onset of charismatic life, or to third and fourth experiences of the Spirit, or any one of a number of varied testimonies.[93] All this is granted. It is unclear, however, what these varieties in current experience and practice affirm or deny. To take an analogy, many are the variations in the testimonies of people *coming to Christ*. Some have known him as their friend all their lives; some come to know him gradually; some come . . . and drift . . . and come again; some enter new phases of this experiential reality in stages. None of this denies that Christian conviction is real or important. So too with testimonies concerning the Holy Spirit. None of the variety denies the reality of a work of the Spirit that does not regenerate, but empowers.

John, Luke, and Paul

Acknowledging, then, that Turner has not successfully undermined Menzies' implicit proposal, I will undertake my own suggestion. From our study of John 20:22, I want to emphasize that John can use Spirit reception language of two distinct experiences in the lives of at least one group of Christ's followers. I find this permissive. Even if he only

92. Compare the wisdom of George Canty: to be baptized in the Spirit "will not make us more effective than others but only more effective than we ourselves would otherwise be" (quoted in Warrington, *Pentecostal Theology*, 116 n. 422). See also Pawson, "Believing in Christ," 46.

93. Turner, *Holy Spirit and Spiritual Gifts*, 165.

referred this dual experience of the Spirit to that first group of disciples (and I am not convinced that he did), he breaks what might otherwise look like a biblical ban on using Spirit reception language today of two distinct experiences in the life of a new believer.

Turning now to Luke and Paul, who only speak of one distinct initiating Spirit reception each, are their differences merely linguistic or deeply conceptual? It is always difficult to answer this question, for we only ever have access to people's language, and not to their thoughts. In other words, all concepts are communicated through words, and so the concepts "lie behind" and are potentially masked by the words. However, the fact that this book has brought to light Luke's ready acknowledgment of the Spirit's work in converts *prior to* what he called their Spirit reception suggests that the differences are primarily linguistic, rather than conceptual. To give an example, if there was a woman known to both Luke and Paul who responded positively to the gospel and came to belief in Christ, but who only some weeks later first experienced exuberant joy and spoke in tongues (let us say), Paul and Luke, perhaps, would simply describe this process differently, while holding to similar conceptual explanations of the event. Luke's *concept* would include the idea that the Spirit was involved throughout the process. The preacher from whom she heard the gospel was Spirit-filled; Jesus opened her heart to the message by his Spirit; perhaps (let us say) a vision played its part in the process, and this was granted to her by the Spirit. And then, weeks later, she received that experience, which would be ongoing, whereby she felt the immediate glorious presence of Jesus in her life, found herself expressing praise and perhaps prophecy in words she had never learned, and discovered in the days ahead that she had a whole new boldness to share her new faith with others. Luke would also relate this further experience to the work of the Spirit, and at this point only would he use the *language* of Spirit reception.

Paul, I suspect, would agree wholeheartedly with all of Luke's insights into the Spirit's work behind the outward human changes in this convert's life, but he would of course use Spirit reception language of her initial change. If so, their differences are purely linguistic. Luke called her later change, whereby she was emboldened and enabled, her reception of the Spirit. His own cautions kept him from referring to the Spirit when describing her earlier reception of the gospel. While Paul called her earlier experiences her reception of the Spirit, we have no New Testament data by which we could begin to guess what if anything Paul would call the latter experience that she had. At this point, we simply need to acknowledge our paucity of data. We face Paul's silence regarding a delay in Christian initiation between people's placing their faith in the Christian gospel and their experiencing a vivid charismatic equipping. If we allow this silence to "speak," then Paul's converts always experienced this equipping at conversion. However, as Fee points out, this is an argument only from silence.[94] Perhaps Paul, like Luke, regarded coming to belief and being charismatically empowered as *normally* and *ideally* coincident chronologically. That is the impression we gain from his letters, certainly. But we do not know. And when we do not know, we should not pretend that we do.

Conclusion

Luke, Paul, and John have different voices, and these must be respected. To listen to them together should not be to drown out one voice with that of another. Neither should their individual characteristics be ignored in some attempt to achieve a ready harmonization. Together, they testify to variety in the works of the Spirit in a convert to Christ. In particular, these various activities can be clustered in a "soteriological" nexus and a "charismatic" nexus. Between them the authors evidence variety in how linguistic terms can be applied to these nexi of activity. With these findings in mind, we can now consider how we Pentecostals today can best put our convictions into words.

PENTECOSTAL NOMENCLATURE

We Pentecostals are relatively uniform in reserving our use of the terms *baptism in the Holy Spirit*, *Spirit baptism*, and the like for the potentially subsequent charismatic equipping that I have been discussing. This is, of course, not to suggest that we do not use other terms as well. Another common expression is *Spirit-filled*. So the question might be asked, "Have you been filled with the Spirit?" just as easily as, "Have you been baptized in the Spirit?" The actual word *receive* is not so often used of the Spirit in this context. This is unsurprising, given our recognition that the Spirit is

94. Fee, *God's Empowering Presence*, 863; Fee, *First Epistle to the Corinthians*, 605 n. 32.

at work in people's conversion, and that this can be referred to as their initial "reception of the Spirit."

We have to acknowledge that we cannot appeal to the Bible for clear precedent for these uses of our language. An appeal to Paul's pneumatology and language for our talk of a person's receiving the Spirit at conversion to grant new life and an appeal to Luke's concepts and language to talk of charismatic empowering as a "Spirit baptism" would be an inaccurate reflection of both their testimonies. Neither can we appeal to John's use and then somehow "paste on" Paul's and Luke's meanings to his two Spirit receptions. But none of this need worry us. Christians use many terms today in ways quite different from the ways they were used in the Scriptures (not even allowing for variety between scriptural authors, and between speakers and writers today). Examples include such basic and frequently used terms as *preach*, *pastor*, and *church*. As long as we acknowledge that we are not using terms quite as biblical authors used them, the terms are available to us for our own use.

I believe it is appropriate for Pentecostals to call that subsequent equipping to which so many testify their "baptism in the Spirit." Paul did not use this term for that experience. The Pentecostal use is closer to Luke's use (though Luke used it little; and modern use individualizes the concept, losing the corporate connotations that may have been important to Luke). But ultimately this matters little. The experience exists.[95] It could be called "empowering with the Spirit," or being "baptized with the power of the Spirit," as I have heard it put. It could be put into terms that do not include the word *Spirit* at all. But "baptism in the Spirit" is a convenient label, adhering firmly to the concept we have in mind through long-established use, widely employed today and widely understood by Pentecostals and non-Pentecostals alike. It might as well remain in place.

CONCLUSIONS

It is most unlikely that either Luke, Paul, or John wrote with the thought, let alone the express intent, that their words should in future times be held alongside those of others from their generation. When we do so, we

---

95. It must, of course, be admitted that nobody can demonstrate that an experience had today is exactly or even approximately the same as one testified to in the New Testament. That parallels exist between the two can be asserted, and on reasonably good grounds, but cannot be proved.

thus engage in an exercise that is most probably artificial from the point of view of their writing. However, we acknowledge the superintendence of the God who inspired their writing. And we dare to believe in God's help in our reading.

It has emerged as we have listened to the New Testament voices of Luke, Paul, and John together that there is variety in how they used Spirit reception language. John could write, by way of promise and record, of the first disciples receiving the Spirit twice, for different purposes. Luke and Paul did not do this. Paul, in contrast to Luke, reserved terms to do with receiving the Spirit—including being baptized with the Spirit—for the saving work of God that brought a person into relationship through Jesus.

Pentecostals have recognized this—and Dunn has misread Pentecostals at this point. Throughout Pentecostal history there has been a recognition of the Spirit's regenerating work. And today's Pentecostal New Testament scholars—the best ones—do not argue with Dunn over his understanding of Paul. But we continue to assert confidently that Luke does not reflect Paul in this particular regard.

It is difficult to bring the voices together. Menzies and Turner have been in friendly dispute over this, but the Pentecostal understanding has not been disproved. There is "room" among the New Testament voices that allows Pentecostals today to talk of a reception of the Spirit whereby converts gain new covenant life in Christ, and a possibly subsequent charismatic equipping that ensures they can play their part in the church's service and mission: their "personal Pentecost"; their "baptism in the Holy Spirit."

5

Baptism in the Spirit Today

SUMMARIES

IN THIS FIRST SECTION, I intend to summarize the findings of each chapter and to draw out any further significant conclusions from these findings. The second, longer, section will then consider practical lessons on the subject that Luke might have to offer today's Pentecostal churches.

Chapter 1

Chapter 1 introduced the key themes and central players in the topic and the debate that this book discusses. We saw the centrality of Spirit baptism to Pentecostalism and the centrality of Luke-Acts in biblical studies supporting this doctrine. We also noted the great importance of James Dunn's part in the debate surrounding Spirit baptism and met the Pentecostals around the debating table facing Dunn. The key work by Dunn is his doctoral thesis, published as *Baptism in the Holy Spirit*, and the key issue under debate is New Testament teaching concerning being baptized in the Holy Spirit. For Dunn, this is the action of God whereby a person turning to Christ in faith is granted God's forgiveness and new covenant life. This is as true of Luke's testimony as it is of any other part of the New Testament. Dunn has held consistently to this view throughout his career, as his occasional further writing on the subject has indicated. Naturally, Dunn is critical of Pentecostal readings of the New Testament that understand being baptized in the Spirit as another distinct act of God by the Spirit that is charismatic and empowering.

Chapter 2

In chapter 2, I assessed the criticisms offered by Dunn's Pentecostal respondents in order to decide whether a cogent refutation is offered to Dunn's views. Turning first to Jesus' reception of the Spirit in Luke, Dunn's critics correctly identify this anointing as an empowering to minister to others (with which point Dunn does not disagree), but are less helpful concerning the epochal and covenantal significance of the event. It must be given its due weight as a significant step in the transition from old to new in Luke's salvation history: only now is God's unique Messiah anointed for his unique task. Dunn is quite wrong, however, to see this event as somehow ushering Jesus into the new covenant. This idea is far from Luke's concepts: Luke offered no suggestion that Jesus even *needed* to be *ushered* into the new covenant. Jesus' explanation will suffice: he was anointed for public liberating ministries (Luke 4:18–21). Luke viewed this anointing on Jesus as in key ways unique, but still, in part, as a pattern for the later Spirit reception that his followers would experience. To this extent, their later reception of the Spirit would not usher them, either, into the new covenant, but rather empower them to follow Jesus' example in fulfilling God's mission to the nations.

Turning now to Acts and first to Pentecost, Dunn's respondents do here successfully dissociate the gift of the Spirit from mediation of the new covenant. They succeed in reflecting more faithfully than Dunn Luke's emphasis on *power* as that which the Spirit brought and highlight Luke's emphasis on the *prophetic* nature of the gift, which was granted to those who were *already* God's servants. This is most important. Acts 1:8 must not be underplayed. The pivotal dominical statement towers over Acts 2 and over subsequent chapters of Acts, all of which must be read in its light.

Turning to those later chapters, and their testimony to the separation in Luke's thought between conversion and Spirit reception, the Samaritan account definitely represents strong ground for Pentecostal doctrine, but it is not an isolated "proof text." In its support, the Cornelius episode indicates that the Spirit's arrival did not bring new covenant life, but granted the outward evidence of what God was doing within. Furthermore, the Ephesian reception shows, most of all through the record of Paul's question, Luke's thought: belief was possible without reception of the Spirit. On all these occasions the recipients were, like the 120 on the day of Pentecost, enabled by the Spirit to engage in charismatic activity. This activity, the earlier programmatic material implies, would help them participate in the church's expanding mission as well as in their own Christian lives.

Chapter 3

Chapter 3 considered Pentecostal alternatives to Dunn's position. Any such alternative that radically separates Spirit baptism from Christian beginnings thereby misrepresents Luke, who programmatically linked the Pentecostal gift of the Spirit to other aspects of Christian initiation through his record of Peter's Pentecost preaching. As Acts 1:8 dominates the book pneumatologically, so does Acts 2:38. We have to assume that Luke expected converts, typically, to receive the Spirit at or near the time of their baptism in water, which was not regarded as an event that would occur months or more after the inception of Christian faith. Delays and other departures from the typical pattern were by no means impossible, but were to be remedied urgently.

When the Spirit did arrive in converts' lives, recipients were enabled to take an effective part in the worldwide evangelistic mission of the growing church. This is admittedly not often evident through a surface reading of the later chapters of Acts. It is the echo of Acts 1:8, supported by Luke 4:18; 12:12; 24:49; Acts 1:1, 4; 2:4, 11; 4:31; 8:1–4; 10:38; 11:19–21; 16:10; etc., which leads to this conclusion. The enabling evidently included: boldness in witness; guidance in the mission; and the ability to heal, to cast out demons, and to perform other miracles. However, this enabling went beyond the church's outward mission. It also clearly included a charismatic enabling to contribute to the guidance of the church in its internal affairs. Furthermore, the Spirit granted recipients the capacity to engage in charismatic praise and offered personal joy and encouragement.

Thus the Spirit's engagement in a Christian life was broad, and Luke knew of no ongoing active Christian life without it. This does not mean, however, that the Spirit was inactive prior to someone's receiving the Pentecostal gift of the Spirit. The Spirit could perform individual acts, such as granting a vision or opening a heart, before the convert actually received the Spirit. So the Spirit was soteriologically involved, but the Pentecostal reception of the Spirit was not soteriological: it was charismatic and missionary. This distinction between prior works of the Spirit and the actual gift of the Spirit in Luke's thinking is important. It provides a first step in the process by which Luke's testimony is brought alongside other New Testament voices for them to be heard together.

Chapter 4

In chapter 4, Luke's voice was brought within hearing of Paul's and John's. Taken together, these authors indicate the variety there is in the New Testament concerning use of Spirit reception language. John could write of the first disciples receiving the Spirit twice, for different purposes. Luke and Paul did not do this, but their references to one Spirit reception were not identical. Today's best Pentecostal New Testament scholars do not argue with Dunn over his understanding of Paul; they simply understand that, at this point, Luke did not reflect Paul. Paul, in contrast to Luke, reserved terms to do with first receiving the Spirit for the inception of a person's relationship through Jesus. Luke, on the other hand, wrote implicitly of the Spirit's work in converts prior to their reception of the Spirit and reserved use of Spirit reception terms for charismatic equipping. No author meant by the term and its variations precisely what the others meant. As Turner observed in 1980, *to receive the Spirit* and similar phrases were not fixed technical terms when the New Testament was being written.[1] They were fluid, and this fluidity is attested in the variety in use between the authors. With this variety in mind, however, it is important to note that Luke's acknowledgement of the Spirit's prior works contributes usefully to a constructive joint hearing of the three authors.

When they are heard together today, without one voice drowning the others out, the variety and implicit underlying flexibility create latitude to speak of a reception of the Spirit that brings someone into new covenant life in Christ and another work of the Spirit for a different purpose that clearly does not necessarily happen at the same time. Luke's portrayal of the church's early life supplies that purpose: it is charismatic and missionary. At the heart of this Lukan portrayal stands a day, and an event, that has given the name to our movement. We recognize that this further work of the Spirit is our personal "Pentecost." We are glad to borrow New Testament language further, and so name this further work of the Spirit. We declare that by God's infinite grace we have been *baptized in the Holy Spirit*.

---

1. Turner, "Luke and the Spirit," 28.

Conclusion

Dunn has much that is useful to offer concerning New Testament views about reception of the Holy Spirit. However, his Pentecostal debaters have shown, overall, that in the case of Luke-Acts Dunn, as Turner exclaimed in 1980,[2] is wrong. Taken together, the Pentecostals under review offer a more cogent reading of Luke-Acts. The strongest Pentecostal views are those that retain a sufficiently broad view of the Spirit's role: this role is primarily prophetic, but this does not exclude works of power; it is primarily for the church's outward mission, but this does not exclude the internal life of the church and its individual members. Also, Pentecostal readings of Luke-Acts that highlight the initiatory aspect of Spirit reception more faithfully reflect Luke's thinking.

Pentecostal attempts to undermine Dunn's exegesis of Paul are doomed to fail. On Paul, to put it equally simply, Dunn is right. For the most part, he is also right concerning John. Less work has been done by these Pentecostals concerning how the New Testament voices can be heard together. When this is attempted, recognition of Luke's "prior works" helps the process considerably. The resultant symphony of New Testament sounds allows a hearing today of two strands, which we Pentecostals can "revocalize" in our talk of two Spirit receptions, the latter of which we call our baptism in the Holy Spirit.

This conclusion that Luke-Acts contributes significantly to a Pentecostal *doctrine* of baptism in the Spirit raises a subsequent question: have Pentecostals sufficiently allowed Luke's data to inform their *practice* concerning receiving the Spirit in this way? In the next section, I will develop some of the practical implications that Luke's portrayal of reception of the Spirit in the earliest church has for Pentecostal life today.

PRACTICAL IMPLICATIONS

As I wrote in chapter 1, it has not been my expectation that this book will sway the views of non-Pentecostals who have studied the subject long and hard and have long since formed clear, stable opinions about the work of the Spirit in Christian beginnings. But to such people I do make an appeal: it is that they *respect* Pentecostal viewpoints as faithful reflections of one way the relevant New Testament documents can be

---

2. See Turner, "James Dunn's *Baptism*," 25.

read.[3] If I might be permitted to appeal to Dunn's advice at this point, he suggests that: "We cannot claim to accept the authority of the NT unless we are willing to accept as valid *whatever* form of Christianity can justifiably claim to be rooted in one of the strands that make up the NT."[4] I think I speak for many Pentecostals in suggesting that we have a relatively strong claim to "be rooted in [at least] one of the strands that make up" the New Testament. The days should be over, if they ever existed, when it can validly be said of Pentecostals by other Christians, "They clearly know God; but they do not know the Bible!"

However, I also made it clear in my introductory remarks to this book that I have written it primarily to my fellow Pentecostals. I believe that Luke-Acts presents us Pentecostals with some highly significant challenges. Before we turn to these practical lessons from Luke's works for today's churches, we need briefly to consider his purpose in writing. This is to gauge whether we can validly draw any lessons from Luke-Acts other than Luke's stated purpose: that carefully researched history of Christianity's beginnings should be known, so as to offer an assurance of the teaching's certainty (Luke 1:1–4).

Luke's Purpose

Though Luke briefly stated his overall purpose for writing, much scholarly attention has been devoted to this question, for Luke's choices of subject matter suggest further subsidiary interests and purposes. Traditional Lukan scholarship has often focused on the apologetic interests that Luke might have had, and considered whether he was offering a defense document for Paul's trials, or more broadly, an apologetic for the church in its conduct with the wider Roman world.[5] These discussions tended to be speculative, and recent discussions have more profitably turned their attention to Luke's pastoral concerns. Luke was clearly writing to Christians, not only to assure them of the firm foundation on which their Christianity stood but also to encourage them to participate in the ongoing mission and to stand up under suffering.[6] Narrowing this

3. An obvious corollary presents itself at this point: Pentecostals should also warmly respect the practical pneumatologies of fellow Christians that are at variance to their own.

4. Dunn, *Unity and Diversity*, 377; italics original.

5. For brief discussion see Guthrie, *New Testament Introduction*, 367–69.

6. See the discussion in Peterson, "Luke's Theological Enterprise," 534–44.

theme, Menzies persuasively contends that Luke was particularly seeking to engage his readers in an ongoing commitment to the mission Luke described in his works. With sustained reference to Luke 10:1–16 and its echoes of Numbers 11:24–30, Menzies sees Luke hoping that all his readers would be prophets and would go out two-by-two on their own missions in continuity with those Luke described. As Menzies convincingly states, "Luke's narrative is far more than a nostalgic review of how it all began . . . The story continues, as the ending of Acts anticipates, with the readers taking up their mantle of ministry modeled by Jesus and his disciples. Luke narrates the story of Jesus and the early church in order to challenge his church (and every church in 'these last days') to take up its prophetic calling by listening to the voice of the Spirit and bearing bold witness for Jesus. Luke's two-volume work is a missions manifesto."[7] Insofar as Pentecostal churches today, in their various contexts, will no doubt share certain areas of common ground with the churches of Luke's day, it is valid for us to follow Menzies and listen to the practical challenges Luke-Acts continues to offer. I will consider several excerpts from Acts for this purpose.

Acts 1:8

As I stated earlier in the book, this verse "towers over" the rest of Acts. It is most important to consider that Luke narrated these words as the *last* ones Jesus spoke prior to his ascension. They are his final earthly promise and implicit instruction. This realization is accentuated by other observations about the narrative structure at this point. Acts 1:1–5 is in effect merely an introductory summary of Luke's first volume. Acts 1:6–7 is also preparatory, in that it presents Jesus' clearing away of misconceptions before he presents his true conception of the situation at that time.[8] Thus, it becomes even clearer how central Acts 1:8 is in Luke's narrative structure and purpose. At this point, given Menzies' reasoning, we can hear not only Jesus' words to his immediate followers, but Luke's words to his readers. By extension, we hear divine words to us.

My first practical concern is with the breadth of the promise to receive power, and therefore of the implicit command to implement it in witness. One must trace back to Acts 1:2 to find a noun that might indi-

---

7. Menzies, "Sending of the Seventy," 91–92.
8. See discussion in May, "Is Luke a Reader-Response Critic?" 75–76, 83.

cate the breadth of hearers to whom Jesus was speaking in Acts 1:8—and it was the apostles. However, it is by no means certain that the noun-phrase "those who had come together" (Acts 1:6) referred only to the apostles. In Luke 24, the similar promise and implicit command (Luke 24:47–49) was offered to a wider group (Luke 24:33). Furthermore, as Luke presented the fulfillment of the promise, it clearly occurred in the lives of the gathered believers (Acts 1:15; 2:1, 4; cf. 4:31), not just of the apostles. This is important as we consider empowerment for evangelism today. According to Turner's reading of Luke-Acts, only a few people were notably influenced by the Spirit, such that Luke would call them "Spirit-filled." "Ordinary" Christians were called merely to be an audience and perhaps support for the few who did the active work of evangelizing. Therefore, by this reading, Luke's readers would face no other personal challenge from Acts than to support the ministry of the few in their day. Menzies' reading is quite different, and more convincing. Implicitly, all of us who read Luke-Acts face the challenge, both to ensure that we have received the power Jesus promised, and to implement that power in witnessing to Jesus.

My second concern is with the content of the promise, and particularly its latter part. The promise that they would be witnesses to the end of the earth involved the breaking of many barriers, as is illustrated so compellingly by the rest of Luke's narrative. The spread of the gospel overcame barriers of language, persecution, travel, resistance, culture, and religion.[9] Implicitly, it overcame "internal" barriers of prejudice, misunderstanding, and perhaps frank cruelty. Some of these were in the attitudes of those who offered the witness and some in those who heard it. Today, there is a challenge in these words to Pentecostal churches and individuals to believe in the capacity of our witness to overcome barriers. However, none of the barriers was overcome simply through the "power" of belief. Luke's narrative records the sheer effort of those who took Jesus' promise seriously and sought to live in its reality. In similar vein, we must make every effort to tear down or climb over the barriers that present themselves to us and take God's great gospel to those who as yet live on the "other side" of these barriers.

9. See, e.g., Warrington, *Message of the Holy Spirit*, 122–25.

Acts 2:38–39

My concern here is with the nature of the evangelistic appeal and promise at Acts 2:38. Dunn asks, "Has modern evangelism held forth the promise of the Spirit explicitly enough?"[10] I echo his concern and extend it to Pentecostal evangelism. Our evangelism should not be silent on the promise of the Spirit. Discussion of baptism in the Spirit should not be reserved for nurture classes or baptismal classes (indeed, whether water baptism should wait until after classes is a question that Luke-Acts raises). Instead, presentations of the gospel from the lips of Pentecostals need to make it clear that part of the promise God offers to those who turn in faith to Christ is that God will grant them the Pentecostal gift of the Spirit.

Our determination to include the Spirit in our evangelistic communication must extend beyond how we present the gospel message. Our ways of assisting those who are making decisions to follow Jesus need to include talk of the Spirit. Specifically, if we are helping them to find words to pray—leading them phrase by phrase in a prayer of commitment, perhaps—this prayer should surely include the appeal to God to send the Spirit in fullness: to flood the person with presence, praise, and power, and to equip the person for active service in God's kingdom and mission.

Acts 4:23–31

The practical challenges issuing from this text relate to prayer. It is instructive that the prayer Luke recorded did not contain a request for God to grant the Spirit. The prayer was for boldness to speak and for healings, signs, and wonders. However, that God's response was to send the Spirit comes as no surprise to those familiar with Lukan pneumatology. We may be permitted to see here, in the absence of a request for the Spirit to come, a selflessness on the part of those who prayed: they were not, perhaps, interested so much in their immediate religious experience as in the need for God's word to be proclaimed without fear and confirmed through acts of divine power.

Beyond that, we need to remember that many of those who were praying were people who had already experienced Pentecost. It is highly instructive that their previous experience did not discourage them from

---

10. Dunn, *Baptism*, 229.

praying for renewed acts of power. In effect, they asked for *more*. We can do no better. Luke did not offer any information at all that coheres with today's testimonies that Christians, so to speak, "leak": that however full of the Spirit one may have been yesterday offers no guarantee for one's spiritual health today. Nonetheless, this prayer alone is an encouragement to keep seeking the fullness of the Spirit. Luke would not encourage any Christian today to be satisfied with "yesterday's manna."

Acts offers earlier help in relation to prayer for the Spirit to come. While in Acts 1:14 Luke wrote that "they were all devoting themselves with one accord to prayer," he did not record the contents of these prayers (in contrast to Acts 4:24–30). However, Luke 11:13; 12:12; 24:49; Acts 1:5, 8 give us due cause to imagine that at least some of their praying on these occasions concerned the promised imminent arrival of God's Spirit, and the opportunity that would immediately follow to know the Spirit's power and guidance as they engaged anew in the mission for which Jesus had commissioned them. I contrast this with repeated experiences in my context, where concentrated prayer for the Spirit to come upon God's people corporately seems largely to be confined either to times when this is what the Spirit is doing anyway or to times when a leader decides that this is how the church should pray. Prayer for outpourings of the Spirit on God's people do not seem to be linked in our minds with organized evangelism. When a mission is planned, perhaps involving several local churches in a town, there is of course prayer, but this prayer concerns the plans themselves: that there should, for instance, be sufficient volunteers—and in my own country, for open-air evangelism, prayer involves considerable concern about the weather! But there seems to be little thought given at these times about the need of the churches for God's Spirit to be poured out upon them in Pentecostal power with the precise purpose of enabling the mission that is being planned. This may be part of a wider divorce in Pentecostal thinking between fullness of the Spirit and evangelism. Perhaps under the influence of newer charismatic and renewal movements, we Pentecostals have contented ourselves with connecting fullness of the Spirit to the immediate religious experience of individual recipients. Luke would not demur (e.g., Acts 10:46). But he would emphasize the broader missionary purpose of the eschatological outpouring of the Spirit. Luke has been echoed in our generation by Colin Dye, a prominent British Pentecostal leader: "This isn't for us; it's

for them!"[11] Are too many Pentecostals praying for the Spirit so that—
to put it bluntly— they *feel* good, rather than primarily for the sake of
those who may never experience real life unless empowered Christians
take God's good news to them? As Dye reminds us elsewhere, "There
is still a very long way to go before the true purpose of Pentecost is re-
established. The Holy Spirit is still being called upon to bring 'a blessing'.
His influences are mainly being seen on the Church. But what about
the lost? What of the harvest? We must ensure the primary focus of our
encounters with the Spirit is to be empowered to reach the lost."[12]

Acts 6:3—7:60

The amazing initial behavior of the 120 when they were filled with the
Spirit on the day of Pentecost was recorded by Luke. On subsequent
occasions too Luke recorded the initial vocal outbursts of recipients
(Acts 10:46; 19:6; cf. 8:18). In turn, we Pentecostals have traditionally
concerned ourselves with what we have called "initial evidence." In the
next section, I will make brief reference to what that "initial evidence"
might be. However, at this stage, I want to discuss something which may
actually have been more important to Luke: *ongoing evidence*. I choose
this section of Acts because, as I observed in chapter 3, Stephen was the
only Christian whose fullness of the Spirit Luke traced through to his
death (Acts 6:5, 10; 7:55). Therefore, here we have a particularly firm
basis for conclusions regarding the ongoing evidence of fullness of the
Spirit in a Christian life. Indeed, as Stronstad indicates, Luke emphasized
Stephen's fullness of the Spirit in more concentrated fashion than with
anyone else except Jesus.[13]

We do not know what the initial evidence was of Stephen's reception of the Spirit, for we do not know if he was one of the 120, but we
certainly know what the ongoing evidence of his fullness of the Spirit
was. And, just as Menzies is right—Luke's account was no mere piece
of nostalgia, but a deliberate challenge to his readers to continue Jesus'
mission—Stronstad is right to deduce that Stephen, like other prominent
characters in Luke's record, typified "the ministry of the prophethood of

---

11. Stated publicly on many occasions in the presence of the author. To be precise,
previous chapters have shown that Luke would declare, "This isn't *primarily* for us, but
for them!"

12. Dye, "Are Pentecostals Pentecostal?" 71.

13. Stronstad, *Prophethood of All Believers*, 87 n. 4, 88.

all believers."[14] So today, we Pentecostals may justifiably stand in awe of the life of Stephen, but we will do well, also, to be challenged: what ongoing evidence is there in our lives that we are filled with the Spirit? It is insufficient for Pentecostals to look back to a point in their personal histories when they spoke in tongues or delighted in praise. The rigorous self-examination in which all Christians must engage includes, in all of us who claim the "charismata" for today, such questions as: "Am I a charismatic prophet?—a bold witness? Do I exude faith and wisdom? Do I see visions or hear from God in direct ways? Do my deeds serve as 'signs'? Am I ready to suffer, even to lay down my life, for my witness to Jesus?" We may not all be as outstanding as Stephen was—and we certainly may not all expect to look like angels! (Acts 6:15)—but that cannot be an excuse. There should surely be clear ongoing evidence in our lives that God's Spirit is within us, empowering us to live effective lives and enabling us to perform successful ministries for God.

Acts 8:14–17

What pastoral concerns might Luke have had in recording the Samaritan incident? Perhaps he hoped that any of his readers encountering a lack of the Spirit's evident arrival in the lives of new converts might follow the example of Peter and John and take equally urgent steps to correct the situation. This possibility raises a concomitant concern. We need to look at new converts with keen eyes and ask, "Is there something missing?" Clearly, that something was missing was evident to the apostles who arrived from Jerusalem that day. Corroborative evidence for this conclusion lies not only in other accounts of Spirit reception in Luke-Acts, but in the account itself: as is well known among Pentecostals, the fact that Simon offered money for the ability to confer the Spirit shows that something dramatic happened when these Samaritans received the Spirit. It must have been the absence of such evidence that alerted the apostles to their need to pray for these people. We need, in love, to look for the presence or absence of charismatic activity in converts' lives and pray concertedly for any who lack this.

Clearly, this raises the question of what was missing and thus of Pentecostal doctrines of speaking in tongues as the initial evidence of

---

14. Ibid., 85. In this work, Stronstad helpfully discusses Stephen's charismatic ministry (ibid., 85–90, 100–101).

baptism in the Spirit. I have so far deliberately avoided this debate. Dunn also avoids it. His only comment in *Baptism* is that, "Pentecostal teaching on spiritual gifts, including glossolalia, while still unbalanced, is much more soundly based on the NT than is generally recognized."[15] He offers somewhat more sustained comments in his *Jesus and the Spirit*. His conclusion is that: "we can hardly doubt that glossolalia was recognized as a manifestation of the Spirit in the earliest days of the church; but that the early believers gave it the significance which modern Pentecostals attach to it is not a conclusion we can justly draw from Luke's account."[16] I agree with him. I must admit that I like the studied vagueness of my own denomination's reference in its statement of beliefs to "baptism in the Holy Spirit with signs following." I appreciate that this leaves open what these signs may be. Luke described several immediate charismatic consequences of receiving the Spirit. As I have already noted (in chapter 2), Dunn is not unwilling to acknowledge this: the arrival of the Spirit in Acts was "dramatic" and "manifest."[17] Speaking in tongues was an important example of these dramatic manifestations, undoubtedly. However, Pentecostal arguments that attempt to draw the conclusion from Acts that *only* speaking in tongues provides adequate evidence that someone has received the Pentecostal gift are not convincing. Pentecostals with pastoral responsibility for new converts may well encourage those converts to seek the capacity to speak in tongues, but any appropriate charismatic activity or ability is surely sufficient evidence that they have experienced their "personal Pentecost." A lack of such evidence, however, must alert these pastors to the need to pray for these people.

Acts 10:44–47

This fascinating incident reminds us Pentecostals, among other things, that God is well able to transcend our boundaries. Here, then, we find strong echoes of the promise in Acts 1:8. Peter's greatest psychological barrier to the incident occurring at all was his attitude to Gentiles (his first words on entering Cornelius' home [Acts 10:28] were hardly a first class example of seeker-sensitive evangelism!). We Pentecostals may find ourselves in situations where we too regard a people-group as somehow

---

15. Dunn, *Baptism*, 229.

16. Dunn, *Jesus and the Spirit*, 193; italics removed.

17. Dunn, *Baptism*, 54, 100.

beyond God's reach. The Holy Spirit has evidently been poured out in the twentieth and twenty-first centuries upon certain church groups that some Pentecostals have regarded with theological suspicion. God breaks human boundaries. We must not call *unclean* what God has declared *clean*.

However, this was not the only boundary that was crossed that day. The more directly pneumatological boundary that God crossed was that the Holy Spirit's arrival in the lives of Cornelius and his friends interrupted the Holy Spirit's work in and through the preaching that Peter was engaged in at the time. One is tempted to opine that this is something that "God would not do." We are well aware, and wisely guided by, Paul's injunction to the Corinthians, in the context of charismatic activity in public worship: "Let all things be done decently and in order" (1 Cor 14:40). We must be careful, however, that our sense of order does not become more restrictive than God's sense of order. It is difficult to imagine an unbiased observer describing the scenes in Cornelius' home as *orderly* (compare the scoffing that occurred on the day of Pentecost— Acts 2:13). Only a spiritual ear attuned to God's voice and ways might be able to identify order in the "chaotic" (in our view) ways that God sometimes acts.[18]

Acts 19:1–6

We cannot be certain whether in Luke's mind the Ephesian twelve were disciples of Apollos or of John the Baptist. More likely, they only knew John's ministry, but we cannot be certain. What is clear is that they had received some teaching before meeting Paul and that the teaching they had earlier received had been good. This is true, whether they learned it from John (perhaps indirectly) or from Apollos. Luke held John up as "more than a prophet" (Luke 7:26), as the hinge between the eras (Luke 16:16), and as the one who made the way for the Lord (Luke 3:4), going out in the spirit and power of Elijah (Luke 1:17). Despite his doubts (Luke 7:18–20), John was clearly, for Luke, a hero. So any teaching he gave the Ephesian twelve, or any teaching that they had gained from him indirectly via his more immediate followers, would in Luke's eyes have been

---

18. Levison is willing to use the word *chaos* repeatedly (Levison, *Filled with the Spirit*, 328–29, 335), including in this flourish of alliteration: Luke in his account of Pentecost "draws the curtain back on the chaos that confronted the coterie that would shortly constitute the church in Jerusalem" (ibid., 328).

good. Equally, if Apollos had taught the Ephesians, the input would have been good, for Apollos taught about Jesus accurately and was fervent in Spirit (Acts 18:25). So the prior teaching these Ephesians had received had been *good*. But it had not been *adequate*. Again, whether from John or from Apollos, their previous teaching displayed significant gaps. If it was from John, they would have heard of the Spirit's future outpouring through the Coming One (Luke 3:16). Their answer to Paul in Acts 19:2 would have meant not that they were ignorant of the Spirit's existence but that they were ignorant of the current availability of the Spirit. They did not know that the promise had yet been fulfilled. If their previous teaching was from Apollos, it had not adequately informed them of the place of the Spirit in a disciple's life. Apollos himself had to be taught the way of God more adequately by Priscilla and Aquila (Acts 18:26).

Today, people come into Pentecostal churches from other backgrounds who have received teaching that has been good, but it has not been adequate. We Pentecostals celebrate all good teaching from the Bible that is offered today, whatever the context. But we have a right to be concerned about teaching that either ignores the place of the Holy Spirit in Christian life and service or actually denies that the Spirit works in manifest, charismatic ways today. Those who have received such teaching may, like the Ephesians, not know that the Spirit is available—in these ways—today.

We Pentecostals have a responsibility towards such people. They will not be like the Ephesians in most respects: I am not trying to draw the parallel too closely. Unlike the Ephesians, they may already be real Christians and have been such for years. But like the Ephesians, they may have had prior teaching that was good, but inadequate. We must make good the gap. Like Paul in Acts 19, we must teach them the "full gospel" and pray for them to receive the Spirit. Whatever our precise theology of Spirit reception, let us pray overtly for such people to receive what has been kept from them through inadequate teaching that has in turn led to inadequate expectations on their part. Our expectations must be higher.

A FINAL WORD

In summary, Luke's narrative of the Spirit's arrival and influence in people's lives continues to present considerable challenges to today's Pentecostal churches. We need to listen to them carefully and act accordingly. Despite the seriousness of these challenges, however, let me end on a positive and reassuring note. We Pentecostals have an understanding of the Spirit's work that is based on a fair and appropriate reading of the New Testament, as well as on a testimony of that work within and among us. Distinctive Pentecostal doctrines have known sharp challenges in the last few decades but have withstood these assaults. We do not need to be ashamed of our beliefs or imagine that they are vulnerable if studied in detail. To you I say, hold your heads up high!

Bibliography

Alexander, Paul, et al., editors. *Trajectories in the Book of Acts*. Eugene, OR: Wipf & Stock, 2010.

Anderson, Allan. *An Introduction to Pentecostalism*. Cambridge: Cambridge University Press, 2004.

Arrington, French. *The Acts of the Apostles: Introduction, Translation and Commentary*. Peabody, MA: Hendrickson, 1988.

Atkinson, William P. "Pentecostal Responses to Dunn's *Baptism in the Holy Spirit*: Luke-Acts." *JPT* 6 (1995) 87–131.

————. "Pentecostal Responses to Dunn's *Baptism in the Holy Spirit*: Pauline Literature." *JPT* 7 (1995) 49–72.

————. "The Prior Work of the Spirit in Luke's Portrayal." *Australasian Pentecostal Studies* 5–6 (2002) 107–14. Online: http://webjournals.alphacrucis.edu.au/.

Barrett, C. K. *A Commentary on the First Epistle to the Corinthians*. 2nd ed. London: A. & C. Black, 1971.

Beasley-Murray, George R. *Baptism in the New Testament*. London: Macmillan, 1962.

Bruce, F. F. *The Book of the Acts*. Revised edition. Grand Rapids: Eerdmans, 1988.

Bruner, Frederick Dale. *A Theology of the Holy Spirit*. London: Hodder & Stoughton, 1970.

Burgess, Stanley M., and Gary B. McGee. *Dictionary of Pentecostal and Charismatic Movements*. Grand Rapids: Zondervan, 1988.

Carson, Donald A., editor. *Teach Us to Pray: Prayer in the Bible and the World*. Grand Rapids: Baker, 1990.

Charlesworth, James H., editor. *The Old Testament Pseudepigrapha*. Vol. 1. New Haven: Yale University Press, 1983.

————. *The Old Testament Pseudepigrapha*. Vol. 2. New York: Doubleday, 1985.

Congar, Yves. *I Believe in the Holy Spirit*. Vol. I: *The Holy Spirit in the "Economy."* Translated by David Smith. London: Chapman, 1983.

Dayton, Donald W. *Theological Roots of Pentecostalism*. Peabody, MA: Hendrickson, 1987.

Dunn, James D. G. *Baptism in the Holy Spirit: A Re-examination of the New Testament Teaching on the Gift of the Spirit in Relation to Pentecostalism Today*. London: SCM, 1970.

————. "Baptism in the Spirit: A Response to Pentecostal Scholarship in Luke-Acts." Originally in *JPT* 3 (1993) 3–27. Reprinted in *The Christ and the Spirit: Volume 2 Pneumatology*, by James Dunn, 222–42. Edinburgh: T. & T. Clark, 1998. (Footnote page numbers refer to the reprint.)

————. "Baptism in the Holy Spirit: Yet Once More." *JEPTA* 18 (1998) 3–25.

————. "Baptism in the Holy Spirit: Yet Once More—Again." *JPT* 19 (2010) 31–42.

————. *Jesus and the Spirit*. London: SCM, 1975.

———. "Pentecost." Originally "Pentecost, Feast of" in *The New Dictionary of New Testament Theology* (1975–78). Reprinted in *The Christ and the Spirit: Volume 2 Pneumatology*, by James Dunn, 210–15. Edinburgh: T. & T. Clark, 1998. (Footnote page numbers refer to the reprint.)

———. "Rediscovering the Spirit (2)." Originally in *Expository Times* 94 (1982–83) 9–18. Reprinted in *The Christ and the Spirit: Volume 2 Pneumatology*, by James Dunn, 62–80. Edinburgh: T. & T. Clark, 1998. (Footnote page numbers refer to the reprint.)

———. *Romans 1–8*. Word Biblical Commentary 38A. Dallas: Word, 1988.

———. "Spirit-and-Fire Baptism." Originally in *Novum Testamentum* 14 (1972) 81–92. Reprinted in *The Christ and the Spirit: Volume 2 Pneumatology*, by James Dunn, 93–102. Edinburgh: T. & T. Clark, 1998. (Footnote page numbers refer to the reprint.)

———. *The Acts of the Apostles*. Epworth Commentaries. Peterborough, UK: Epworth, 1996.

———. *The Christ and the Spirit: Volume 2 Pneumatology*. Edinburgh: T. & T. Clark, 1998.

———. "'They Believed Philip Preaching' (Acts 8.12): A Reply." Originally in *Irish Biblical Studies* 1 (1979) 175–83. Reprinted in *The Christ and the Spirit: Volume 2 Pneumatology*, by James Dunn, 216–21. Edinburgh: T. & T. Clark, 1998. (Footnote page numbers refer to the reprint.)

———. *Unity and Diversity in the New Testament*. 2nd ed. London: SCM, 1990.

Dye, Colin. "Are Pentecostals Pentecostal? A Revisit to the Doctrine of Pentecost." *JEPTA* XIX (1999) 56–80.

Elbert, Paul. "An Observation on Luke's Composition and Narrative Style of Questions." *Catholic Biblical Quarterly* 66 (2004) 98–109.

———, editor. *Essays on Apostolic Themes: Studies in Honor of Howard M. Ervin*. Peabody, MA: Hendrickson, 1985.

Ervin, Howard M. *Conversion-Initiation and the Baptism in the Holy Spirit: An Engaging Critique of James D. G. Dunn's Baptism in the Holy Spirit*. Peabody, MA: Hendrickson, 1984.

———. *Spirit-Baptism: A Biblical Investigation*. Peabody: Hendrickson, 1987 (1968 as *These Are Not Drunken, As Ye Suppose*).

Everts, Janet Meyer. "The Pauline Letters in James D. G. Dunn's *Baptism in the Holy Spirit*." *JPT* 19 (2010) 12–18.

Fee, Gordon D. *Galatians: Pentecostal Commentary*. Pentecostal Commentary Series. Blandford Forum, UK: Deo, 2008.

———. *God's Empowering Presence*. Peabody, MA: Hendrickson, 1994.

———. *Gospel and Spirit*. Peabody, MA: Hendrickson, 1991.

———. *The First Epistle to the Corinthians*. NICNT. Grand Rapids: Eerdmans, 1987.

———. "Why Pentecostals Read Their Bibles Poorly—and Some Suggested Cures." *JEPTA* 24 (2004) 4–15.

Ferguson, Sinclair B., and David F. Wright, editors. *New Dictionary of Theology*. Leicester, UK: InterVarsity, 1988.

Fitzmyer, Joseph A. *The Gospel according to Luke I–IX*. Anchor Bible 28. New York: Doubleday, 1981.

Frodsham, Stanley H. *Smith Wigglesworth: Apostle of Faith*. London: Elim, 1949.

Green, Michael. *I Believe in the Holy Spirit*. London: Hodder & Stoughton, 1975.

Guthrie, Donald. *New Testament Introduction*. 4th ed. Leicester, UK: Apollos, 1990.

Haya-Prats, Gonzalo. *Empowered Believers: The Holy Spirit in the Book of Acts*. Translated by Scott A. Ellington. Eugene, OR: Cascade Books, 2010.

Heron, Alasdair I. C. *The Holy Spirit*. London: Marshall, Morgan, & Scott, 1983.

Hill, David. *Greek Words and Hebrew Meanings*. 1967. Reprint, Eugene, OR: Wipf & Stock, 2000.

Holdcroft, L. Thomas. *The Holy Spirit: A Pentecostal Interpretation*. Springfield, MO: Gospel, 1962.

Horton, Stanley M. *What the Bible Says about the Holy Spirit*. Springfield, MO: Gospel, 1976.

Hunter, Harold D. *Spirit Baptism: A Pentecostal Alternative*. 1998Reprint. Eugene, OR: Wipf and Stock, 2009.

Irish, Charles M. "Blessed Trinity Society." In *Dictionary of Pentecostal and Charismatic Movements*, edited by Stanley M. Burgess and Gary B. McGee, 89–90. Grand Rapids: Zondervan, 1988.

Jeremias, Joachim. *New Testament Theology*. Vol. 1. London: SCM, 1971.

Lampe, G. W. H. *The Seal of the Spirit*. 1951. Reprint, Eugene, OR: Wipf & Stock, 2004.

Levison, John R. *Filled with the Spirit*. Grand Rapids: Eerdmans, 2009.

MacArthur, John F., Jr. *Charismatic Chaos*. Grand Rapids: Zondervan, 1992.

Macchia, Frank D. *Baptized in the Spirit: A Global Pentecostal Theology*. Grand Rapids: Zondervan, 2006.

———. "Salvation and Spirit Baptism: Another Look at James Dunn's Classic." *Pneuma* 24.1 (2002) 1–6.

Marshall, I. Howard. *Luke: Historian and Theologian*. 3rd ed. Carlisle, UK: Paternoster, 1988.

Marshall, I. Howard, and David Peterson, editors. *Witness to the Gospel: The Theology of Acts*. Grand Rapids: Eerdmans, 1998.

May, Jordan Daniel. "Is Luke a Reader-Response Critic? Luke's Aesthetic Trajectory of Isaiah 49.6 in Acts 13.47." In *Trajectories in the Book of Acts*, edited by Paul Alexander et al., 59–86. Eugene, OR: Wipf & Stock, 2010.

Menzies, Robert P. *Empowered for Witness: The Holy Spirit in Luke-Acts*. JPTSup 6. Sheffield: Sheffield Academic, 1994.

———. "Luke's Understanding of Baptism in the Holy Spirit: A Pentecostal Perspective." *PentecoStudies* 6.1 (2007) 108–26.

———. *The Development of Early Christian Pneumatology with Special Reference to Luke-Acts*. JSNTSup 54. Sheffield: Sheffield Academic, 1991.

———. "The Distinctive Character of Luke's Pneumatology." *Paraclete* 25.4 (1991) 17–30.

———. "The Sending of the Seventy and Luke's Purpose." In *Trajectories in the Book of Acts*, edited by Paul Alexander et al., 87–113. Eugene, OR: Wipf & Stock, 2010.

Menzies, William W. "The Methodology of Pentecostal Theology: An Essay on Hermeneutics." In *Essays on Apostolic Themes: Studies in Honor of Howard M. Ervin*, edited by Paul Elbert, 1–14. Peabody, MA: Hendrickson, 1985.

Michaels, J. Ramsey. "Luke-Acts." In *Dictionary of Pentecostal and Charismatic Movements*, edited by Stanley M. Burgess and Gary B. McGee, 544–61. Grand Rapids: Zondervan, 1988.

Mittelstadt, Martin William. *Reading Luke-Acts in the Pentecostal Tradition*. Cleveland, TN: CPT, 2010.

Montague, George T. *Holy Spirit: Growth of a Biblical Tradition*. New York: Paulist, 1976.

Moo, Douglas J. *The Epistle to the Romans*. NICNT. Grand Rapids: Eerdmans, 1996.

Moule, C. F. D. *An Idiom Book of New Testament Greek*. 2nd ed. Cambridge: Cambridge University Press, 1959.

Nolland, John. *Luke 1—9:20*. Word Biblical Commentary 35A. Dallas, TX: Word, 1989.

O'Neill, J. C. *The Theology of Acts in Its Historical Setting*. 2nd ed. London: SPCK, 1970.

Pawson, David. "Believing in Christ and Receiving the Spirit: A Response to Max Turner." *JPT* 15 (1999) 33–48.

———. *The Normal Christian Birth*. London: Hodder & Stoughton, 1989.

Penney, John Michael. *The Missionary Emphasis of Lukan Pneumatology*. JPTSup 12. Sheffield, UK: Sheffield Academic, 1997.

Peterson, David. "Luke's Theological Enterprise: Integration and Intent." In *Witness to the Gospel: The Theology of Acts*, edited by I. Howard Marshall and David Peterson, 521–44. Grand Rapids: Eerdmans, 1998.

Petts, David. "The Baptism in the Holy Spirit in Relation to Christian Initiation." MTh thesis, University of Nottingham, 1987.

Schweizer, Eduard. *The Holy Spirit*. Translated by R. H. Fuller and I. Fuller. Philadelphia: Fortress, 1980.

Shelton, James B. *Mighty in Word and Deed*. Peabody, MA: Hendrickson, 1991.

Smail, Tom A. *Reflected Glory*. London: Hodder & Stoughton, 1975.

Stronstad, Roger. *Baptized and Filled with the Holy Spirit*. Springfield, MO: Africa's Hope, 2004.

———. "Forty Years On: An Appreciation and Assessment of *Baptism in the Holy Spirit* by James D. G. Dunn." *JPT* 19 (2010) 3–11.

———. "On Being Baptized in the Holy Spirit: A Lukan Emphasis." In *Trajectories in the Book of Acts*, edited by Paul Alexander et al., 160–93. Eugene, OR: Wipf & Stock, 2010.

———. *The Charismatic Theology of St. Luke*. Peabody, MA: Hendrickson, 1984.

———. *The Prophethood of all Believers: A Study in Luke's Charismatic Theology*. JPTSup 16. Sheffield, UK: Sheffield Academic, 1999 (1998).

———. "Unity and Diversity: New Testament Perspectives on the Holy Spirit." *Paraclete* 23.3 (1989) 15–28.

Summers, Ray. *Commentary on Luke*. Waco, TX: Word, 1972.

Synan, Vinson. *An Eyewitness Remembers the Century of the Holy Spirit*. Grand Rapids: Baker, 2010.

Thiselton, Anthony C. *The Two Horizons*. Exeter, UK: Paternoster, 1980.

Thomas, John Christopher. "A Celebration of and Engagement with James D. G. Dunn's *Baptism in the Holy Spirit* Forty Years On." *JPT* 19 (2010) 19–24.

Turner, Max. "Does Luke Believe Reception of the 'Spirit of Prophecy' Makes All 'Prophets'? Inviting Dialogue with Roger Stronstad." *JEPTA* 20 (2000) 3–24.

———. *The Holy Spirit and Spiritual Gifts: Then and Now*. Carlisle: Paternoster, 1996.

———. "James Dunn's *Baptism in the Holy Spirit*: Appreciation and Response." *JPT* 19 (2010) 25–31.

———. "Luke and the Spirit: Studies in the Significance of Receiving the Spirit in Luke-Acts." PhD diss., Cambridge University, 1980.

———. *Power from on High: The Spirit in Israel's Restoration and Witness in Luke-Acts*. JPTSup 9. Sheffield, UK: Sheffield Academic, 1996.

———. "Prayer in the Gospels and Acts." In *Teach Us to Pray: Prayer in the Bible and the World*, edited by D. A. Carson, 58–83. Grand Rapids: Baker, 1990.

———. "The Spirit and the Power of Jesus' Miracles in the Lucan Conception." *Novum Testamentum* 33 (1991) 124–52.

———. "The Spirit of Prophecy and the Power of Authoritative Preaching in Luke-Acts: A Question of Origins." *New Testament Studies* 38 (1992) 66–88.

———. "The 'Spirit of Prophecy' as the Power of Israel's Restoration and Witness." In *Witness to the Gospel: The Theology of Acts*, edited by I. Howard Marshall and David Peterson, 327–48. Grand Rapids: Eerdmans, 1998.

Twelftree, Graham H. *People of the Spirit: Exploring Luke's View of the Church*. London: SPCK, 2009.

Vermes, Geza. *The Complete Dead Sea Scrolls in English*. London: Penguin, 1998.

Ward, Julian W. "Pentecostalist Theology." In *New Dictionary of Theology*, edited by Sinclair B. Ferguson and David F. Wright, 502–5. Leicester, UK: IVP, 1988

Warrington, Keith. *The Message of the Holy Spirit*. The Bible Speaks Today. Downers Grove, IL: InterVarsity, 2009.

———. *Pentecostal Theology: A Theology of Encounter*. London: T. & T. Clark, 2008.

Wenham, John. *Redating Matthew, Mark, & Luke: A Fresh Assault on the Synoptic Problem*. London: Hodder & Stoughton, 1991.

———. *The Elements of New Testament Greek*. Cambridge: Cambridge University Press, 1965.

Wenk, Matthias. *Community-Forming Power: The Socio-Ethical Role of the Spirit in Luke-Acts*. JPTSup 19. Sheffield, UK: Sheffield Academic, 2000.

Williams, J. Rodman. "Baptism in the Holy Spirit." In *Dictionary of Pentecostal and Charismatic Movements*, edited by Stanley M. Burgess and Gary B. McGee, 40–48. Grand Rapids: Zondervan, 1988.

Witherington, Ben, III. *The Acts of the Apostles: A Socio-Rhetorical Commentary*. Grand Rapids: Eerdmans, 1998.

Subject Index

Abraham, 82
Adam, new. *See* New Adam
Age, church. *See* Church age
Age, new. *See* New messianic era
Age, old. *See* Old epoch
Age of the Spirit, 10
Ananias, 12–13, 29, 40, 46, 89
Ananias and Sapphira, 35
Angels, 86–87
Anna, 50
Anti-Pentecostalism, 16, 36–37
Apollos, 30, 55, 65, 109, 136–37

Baptism in water, 14, 30, 41, 44, 48,
    59, 64–65, 68–69, 81, 86–87,
    89, 97
Blessed Trinity Society, 105

Canon-within-the-canon, 5, 92
Charismatic pneumatology, 70–73,
    115–16, 118, 123, 125
Church, 99–100, 127–29
Church age, 10, 125
Cleansing. *See* Purging
Coming One, 33, 56–57, 59
Commissioning, 77
Conversion-initiation, 10, 27, 42,
    62, 93
Cornelius, 13, 36, 45–46, 54–56, 67,
    86, 124, 136
Covenant, new. *See* New covenant
Covenant, old. *See* Old covenant

Day of Pentecost. *See* Pentecost,
    day of
Doctrine of Subsequence. *See*
    Subsequence, doctrine of

Elijah, 136
Elizabeth, 50, 80–81
Ephesian twelve, 14, 28–30, 36, 41,
    43, 45–46, 65, 67–68, 77–78,
    109, 124, 136–37
Epoch, new. *See* New messianic era
Evangelism. *See* Mission,
    evangelistic

Flesh, 103
Forgiveness, 13, 43, 60, 66, 75
Foursquare gospel, 3

Glossolalia, 43, 133, 135

Healing, 74–75, 77, 83
Hermeneutics, 20, 37–38, 102

Illegitimate identity transfer, 27
Initial evidence, 133, 135
Isaac, 82

John the Baptist, 8–9, 14, 30, 33–34,
    41, 45, 50, 56–59, 75, 80–82,
    97, 105, 109, 136–37
Jordan anointing, 8–9, 14, 28–30,
    39, 44–45, 51–52, 81
Joseph, 50, 82
Joy, 33, 77

145

Author Index

Ancient Document Index

Luke (cont.)

Acts (cont.)

20:37	78
21:4	77
21:11	77, 85–86
22:14–15	13
22:16	12
22:19–20	40
24:14	39
26:6	10
26:16–18	13, 86
28:8	77

Romans

6:3–5	99
8	100, 104
8:9	93–94, 100–101, 104, 106, 109–10
8:14	31

1 Corinthians

1:12–15	99
10:1–2	98–99
12:3	39
12:9	97–98
12:12	99
12:13	5–6, 93–100
12:13a	94–97, 99
12:13c	95–97
12:14	99
14:40	136

2 Corinthians

1:21–22	100
3:16–17	103

Galatians

3:27–29	99
4:6	103

Ephesians

1:13–14	100

Colossians

4:11–14	49
4:14	4

Philemon

24	4

DEAD SEA SCROLLS

Entire corpus	34, 53

1QS

4:15, 21	58

1QSb

5:24–25	58

RABBINIC WRITINGS

Entire corpus	58

Numbers Rabbah

15:25	50